POTLATCH

NATIVE CEREMONY AND MYTH ON THE NORTHWEST COAST

MARY GIRAUDO BECK

ILLUSTRATED BY MARVIN OLIVER

ALASKA NORTHWEST BOOKS™

ANCHORAGE • PORTLAND

*To those who have
celebrated the potlatch—
today and yesterday*

Fourth printing 2002

Library of Congress Cataloging-in-Publication Data
    Beck, Mary Giraudo, 1924-
        Potlatch: Native ceremony and myth on the Northwest Coast /
    by Mary Giraudo Beck; illustrations by Marvin Oliver.
        p.   cm.
    Includes bibliographical references (p.126).
    ISBN 0-88240-440-7
    1. Potlatch. 2. Indians of North America—Northwest Coast of
North America—Rites and ceremonies. 3. Indians of North
America—Northwest Coast of North America—Legends. I. Title.
E78.N78B43 1993   92-47012
394.2'089'974—dc20   CIP

Managing Editor: Ellen Harkins Wheat
Manuscript Editor: Lorna Price
Cover and Book Designer: Elizabeth Watson
Illustrations by Marvin Oliver
Cover illustration: Section of *Raven and Sun with Two Frogs*, 1993, painted
wood sculpture 25 feet tall, Tokushima, Japan. Marvin Oliver.

Alaska Northwest Books™
An imprint of Graphic Arts Center Publishing Company
P.O. Box 10306, Portland, OR 97296-0306
503-226-2402
www.gacpc.com

Printed in the United States of America

CONTENTS

ACKNOWLEDGMENTS

I would like to express appreciation to Gilbert McCleod, Bob Henning, and Ivy and Robert Peratrovich for providing information, and to Andrew Hope III for recommending sources.

I am grateful too to Dolly Jensen and Nancy and Jonathan DeWitt for reading the manuscript for authenticity and also supplying information.

My special thanks go to editors Ellen Wheat and Lorna Price for their invaluable suggestions on the text.

INTRODUCTION

Today totem pole raisings or memorial celebrations are the chief occasions for potlatches, when the people of the Pacific Northwest Coast Native communities gather to celebrate their culture. Songs, dances, and stories enacted in ceremonial regalia remind them of their history and beliefs. Preparations made beforehand—carving the totem, refurbishing ceremonial garments, practicing songs, dances, and stories—stir pride in their traditions and heritage.

For centuries Pacific Northwest Coast peoples from Alaska, Canada, Washington, and Oregon have held potlatches to honor the dead and sometimes also to celebrate births and marriages. These elaborate ceremonies employed complex symbolism and included singing, dancing, recitations of lineages and rights, distribution of gifts, and hosting a lavish feast. Invited guests witnessed these activities and thereby validated their hosts' claims to names, rank, and property. But the claims of the guests to their own rank and prestige were enhanced through the honor accorded them in the position of their assigned seats and the value of the gifts they received, both being determined by the individual's wealth and status.

Athapaskans, Tlingit, Tsimshian, Haida, Kwakiutl, Bella Bella, Bella Coola, West Coast (Nootka), Salish, Makah, Quinault, Chinook—all celebrated the potlatch, each with its own variations on the order or number of the basic elements of singing, dancing, recitations, gift-giving, and feasting, but always observing certain established procedures. Each group had its own name for this ceremony—the Salish *Klanax*, the Tlingit *Xu'ix*, or the Kwakiutl *P!Esa'*. But in communicating with whites or with Natives who spoke a different language, they adopted the Chinook potlatch derived from the West Coast *patshatl*, or "giving."

Today's potlatch, usually of one or two days' duration, is a shortened form of a lavish ceremony that reached the peak of ostentatious luxury in the mid to late nineteenth century. The Natives' wealth, which had increased through trade with Europeans at that time, enabled them to make greater expenditures on increasingly elaborate potlatches.

For Southeast Alaska Natives, honoring the dead was the main purpose of major potlatches and a vital part of any type of potlatch. The Tlingit especially were responsible for the formalization of the cremation and memorial potlatches in the early nineteenth century, and the more formal procedures were gradually adopted by other Pacific Northwest Coast groups. At midcentury this same form carried over to the prestige potlatch, a ceremony with the same basic elements as the funeral potlatch but with added features.

The first of the two potlatches held to honor the dead, the solemn smoking feast and cremation rites, or feeding of the dead, took place right after the death of a high-ranking person. About a year later a second funeral service, the memorial potlatch, was held—a formal eight-day ceremony that served the added purpose of naming the successor chief. Those who could not afford to give the large memorial potlatch, however, could memorialize their recent dead at a major potlatch by donating a gift to it. But ever-increasing wealth gave rise to the prestige potlatch, whose main purpose was to raise the status of children. Only high-ranking, wealthy chiefs could afford to give these luxurious potlatches to further their children's prospects of becoming chief of a house or even head chief of a clan. The less affluent, emulating them, sometimes impoverished themselves in the process.

To possess high status in Northwest Coast Native societies, in addition to being born in a powerful family and clan, one had also to observe social customs and be accomplished in seamanship, fishing, hunting, and waging war. People closely related to the chief had high status, while those more distantly related held middle rank. The very poor and freed slaves made up the lowest class. A chief was selected from the highest ranking nephews of the deceased chief, his sisters' children who, in addition to the traits that earned them high rank, showed strength of character, an even temperament, and high regard for clan tradition.

Major potlatches frequently included some functions of minor ones—dedicating a new house, raising a totem pole, or bestowal of a new name. A new house was built for an anniversary potlatch, and after its dedication the deceased chief's successor would live there with his family. A mortuary pole was raised to memorialize the deceased chief, whose ashes were placed in a box on top or in a niche at the back of the pole. Other poles were raised for prestige purposes. All of them told stories belonging to the clan of the honored person. A pole could also be raised to ridicule someone who had failed to fulfill an agreement or pay a debt, and would depict the specific event. The small potlatches given for these purposes lasted a day or two and generally provided an opportunity to repay debts for services. A small potlatch for women celebrated the coming-out of a young girl who had gone into the customary three-month seclusion at the arrival of her first menses.

An important Pacific Northwest Coast ritual similar to the potlatch and often casually called by that name was the Deer Ceremony, given to solemnize peace treaties. Though this ritual, like a major potlatch, lasted eight days and ended with a feast, it did not include gift-giving or games, and the songs and dances were performed only by the hostages, or "deer"—prominent people carefully selected from the two peace-seeking clans to enact the peace overtures.

A major potlatch, such as the memorial for a deceased chief, lasted eight days. Before the formal ritual of the potlatch, guests were entertained for four days at parties given by various houses of the host clan. The serious rituals of the potlatch then began, and everyone joined the host group in mourning the deceased chief, while the host chief sang mourning songs, repeated clan history and stories, and reiterated clan rights. At this time they also narrated the feats of the clever and wily Raven, a near-deity whom all clans revered for his many gifts to mankind. For it was Raven who had created human beings from lesser creatures and animals from inanimate objects, assigning all their respective roles, and who then gave them the unsurpassed benefits of light, fire, and water. The Tlingit credited their custom of gift-giving to Raven's example.

After the stories came the formal distribution of gifts to all guests, and finally an elaborate feast. In the last days of the potlatch, guests showed their appreciation to the hosts by entertaining them with songs and dances.

Most Pacific Northwest Coast Native societies are divided into clanlike units, but in Tlingit society these clans are divisions of two major social groups, or phratries—the Eagle and the Raven. Membership in a phratry is matrilineal, determined from the mother's line, as are family relationships. Blood relationships are reckoned only between a person and his or her mother's kin. Marriage within the phratry is forbidden; an Eagle always marries a Raven and vice versa.

For funeral and anniversary ceremonies, host potlatch groups employed a clan from the opposite phratry to build the house and to carve and raise the pole. Similarly, a clan from the opposite phratry prepared the body of the deceased, built the pyre, and did all physical work related to the funeral rites. Potlatch guests were clans from the opposite phratry, generally those who had performed some service for the host clan.

Social structure was affected by the interaction of clans both within the village and from other sites as they gathered for the potlatch. In the welcoming ceremony, important chiefs were recognized first, then others according to their standing. The social and political hierarchy within and among clans was further reinforced by protocol that recognized an individual's wealth and clan status to determine seating arrangement and the value of gifts each received, both of which added to the wealth and status of the already rich and powerful.

But it was the association of clans and chiefs with their illustrious ancestors that set a firm seal on the already entrenched aristocracy. For the potlatch, no matter what its occasion, was always a commemoration of the dead, whose spirits were present and took part in the ceremonies. The chiefs' recitations of lineages and early historical events provided strong links between the living and the dead and perpetuated the beliefs and traditions originated by clan forebears. The chief also restated clan rights to property, including fishing and hunting areas, houses and ancestral artifacts, and crests, titles, songs, dances, and stories. The linkage with deceased ancestors added supernatural validation to the host clan's political and ownership rights—rights further secured by the guests' witness to their public reiteration. Such strong influences solidly established the social standing of the chiefs and clans.

Potlatch distribution of wealth came with an obligation to make twofold repayment, which also contributed to the economic activity of Native society by keeping goods circulating and by motivating their production for the ceremonies. In addition, the displays of wealth at potlatches and the giving of gifts encouraged the arts. Much ceremonial regalia was needed. Helmets and frontal pieces for headgear had to be carved; the headgear itself had to be assembled from ermine and eagle feathers and down; staffs had to be carved and drums made and decorated. For ceremonial wear as well as for gifts, blankets were made, jewelry created, and hats were woven and sometimes painted. Boxes and dishes for serving food at the feast or for gifts were also carved. Host and guest clans kept busy with creative activity in the year-long interval between the funeral and anniversary potlatches.

After the turn of the century, the excessively lavish potlatch became an anomaly. Missionary influence, supported in Canada by a law banning potlatches, not only discouraged giving them, but also tended to suppress Native arts, songs, dances, and even Native languages. Later, formation of the Native Brotherhood and Sisterhood associations, along with the rescinding of Canada's anti-potlatch law, encouraged a renewed respect for Native culture among Natives and non-Natives alike. The awakening in the 1960s of public interest in ethnic and especially Native

American cultures gave further impetus to the resurgence of the potlatch and its accompanying arts. Such interest rallied support for the training of carvers and storytellers and for introducing Native culture classes into elementary and high school curriculums.

Although today's potlatches, often called parties, follow the same basic procedures of their more elaborate predecessors, the ceremonies now generally last only one or two days. And potlatches no longer exert the influence they had in former times on the social, political, economic, and legal systems of the community. Yet potlatches still unite Pacific Northwest Coast peoples in the centuries-old celebration of a cultural identity and heritage, as they witness or take part in the traditional songs, dances, stories, speeches, and works of art that make up the event. Non-Natives are often invited to attend potlatch celebrations.

In hopes of bringing interested persons to a fuller appreciation of the present-day potlatch, this book describes the various kinds of major potlatches of the nineteenth century in the longer, more elaborate forms. While the potlatch traditions discussed here were adapted and used by many Pacific Northwest Coast groups, the cultural touchstone of this story is Tlingit. The potlatch today continues to provide a journey into an earlier world, one made livable by the largesse and ingenuity of a beneficent but capricious Raven and by a complex culture and ritual observed by the people of the time to maintain order in their lives.

Raven Survives

R aven was the nephew of Nascakiyel, the first of all beings. Before Raven was born, his mother, Nascakiyel's sister, had given birth to many children, but all died when they were very young. It was believed that Nascakiyel destroyed them for fear that one of his nephews would grow up and replace him as supreme being. The mother cried continually for her lost children.

Heron, Nascakiyel's first creation, was moved by the grieving woman's tears and sought to console her.

"Go down to the beach at the lowest tide and get a small smooth stone," he told her. "Put the stone into the fire to heat, and then swallow it."

The woman followed Heron's directions. Soon she became pregnant and gave birth to Raven. Having a rock for an ancestor made Raven tough and hard to kill.

Nascakiyel realized that Raven was not like his sister's other children and so made him chief of the world.

Raven tried to create mankind from rocks and from leaves. Those created from leaves developed more quickly and peopled the earth. But like the leaves, they also died and returned to the earth more easily.

Raven also made the winds. He commanded the west wind to be gentle, but ordered the south wind to blow hard when it came over the hills. The north wind he put inside a house of ice on top of a snow-covered mountain.

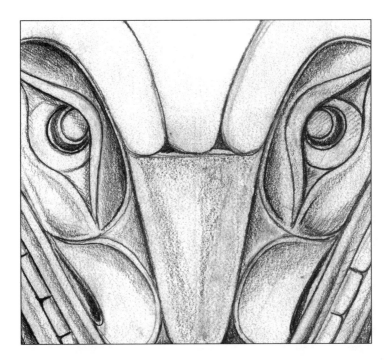

CREMATION AND SMOKING FEAST

T he Grizzly Bear clan chief had just died and the wailing of the women sounded throughout the village. Grizzly Bear women who were close relatives of the chief had cut their hair or singed it and darkened their faces with soot to keep watch over the body. They now loudly mourned his passing. Kowishte, the chief's successor, had called together the brothers and sisters of the deceased chief to make plans for the tobacco and cremation potlatch.

The solemn tobacco feast, eight days of mourning and singing of ancestral songs, was followed by the cremation ceremony. Then all were invited to a feast and smoking ritual, after which the clan that had prepared the chief's body for viewing and conducted the cremation were paid for their services. The Grizzly Bear people would remain silent during the entire ceremony.

The deceased chief's brothers and sisters, distinguished members of the Grizzly Bear clan, called in the Frog clan relatives of the dead chief's wife to arrange the funeral. As her close relatives, they could be trusted by the Grizzly Bears to treat the chief's body with respect. This trust raised the Frog clan and family status, and performing the duties would also increase their wealth and political position. But the chief's brothers themselves would oversee the cremation rite.

Once the Frog clan women arrived, they quickly set about washing the body and preparing it for viewing. They dressed the body in the chief's skin shirt painted with the clan Grizzly Bear and then spread across his legs the Chilkat blanket woven with the clan Killer Whale pattern. They colored his face with red ochre, and on his head they placed his ermine headdress with the Eagle frontlet.

The deceased chief's body was propped in a sitting position against the back wall of the house opposite the door, surrounded by his personal and clan possessions. Displaying his body amid the clan's wealth and symbols of authority not only enhanced his own and his family and clan's social status, but also attested to their political power, origins, and ownership of certain crests and stories. At the chief's right stood the Killer Whale staff, the clan sceptre, and at his left, the bear, a stuffed bear representing the legendary original that had saved them during the Great Flood. Also displayed were wooden hats carved in the form

14

of killer whales, multiple-ringed woven hats, and boxes and baskets of all kinds. Behind him hung another Chilkat blanket and on either side of it, a bear screen and an octopus bag. The deceased chief's wife, wearing her ceremonial button blanket and woven Killer Whale hat, stood in silence next to the body for the mourning. No one was allowed to address her, as she had to remain silent for eight days after her husband's death.

Relatives and friends came to pay their respects. First the Grizzly Bear clan had come, each house leader bearing blankets and other gifts, which were displayed on a long table. Then, summoned by the *nakani*, highly esteemed brothers of the dead chief's wife, the Frog people entered to join in the mourning and to conduct the burial preparations and ceremony.

The new Grizzly Bear chief had squatted with other men of his clan around the fireplace and looked up at the women sitting along the walls. To keep out any possible intruders during the eight nights of mourning, twelve Grizzly Bear men stood guard by the door, beating time with their poles. A group of women, close relatives of the deceased, acted as official mourners while everyone sang the clan's mourning and death songs. The women swayed in rhythm to the singing, rocking with their knees and bending their upper bodies in a graceful movement.

Cremation took place early on the ninth day. While the Frog clan men removed part of the back wall of the house for an opening, Frog clan women took the ceremonial garments off the body and wrapped it in cloths. Then, through the newly made opening, the body was carried on a taut blanket by men of the Frog clan who were close relatives of the widow. It was followed by a dog, which was unceremoniously thrown out, to take with it any trace of illness and spirit influence that had caused the chief's death. Behind the house in which the body had been lying, a funeral pyre had been prepared by the nakani. Over five cedar logs lying side-by-side on the ground, other logs had been set in so as to create a place for the body in the center. Into this opening the men lowered the chief's body, placing over it several woolen blankets and finally the Chilkat blanket that had been spread over his knees at the viewing. Then they covered the opening with cedar logs.

Next five slaves were brought forward. Each was dispatched by a sharp blow to the head with a "slave killer," a picklike wooden tool carved with the clan Shark crest, and their bodies were thrown onto the pyre to burn with their chief. Such a death was regarded as an honor for the slaves. Chosen to accompany their master and serve him in his new life, they earned the distinction of a chief's funeral instead of the slave's rite of being thrown into the sea. At the anniversary potlatch, however, two slaves would be freed in the dead chief's memory.

The people gathered around the pyre were invited to smoke the pipe of tobacco, which was passed around the circle two or three times. Then, at a secret signal from one of the chief's brothers, the pyre was lit. Men and women sat around the pyre, while the male singers stood in a row at its foot, singing and pounding the floorboard at their feet with their staffs. When the singing ended, the mourners left, but a few Frog clan men stayed to tend the bright flames of the pyre. Hours later, after it had burned down and the embers were put out, Frog clan women returned to pick up the ashes and charred bones. These they wrapped in a cloth and placed in a small carved box, to be put in a niche on a mortuary pole carved with the clan crest figures and raised in front of the house built for that purpose.

When the fire was extinguished, the hosts washed the soot from their faces and invited everyone to a feast, where first the feeding of the dead took place. The nakani called out the names of everyone who had brought gifts to be distributed and told what each had donated. Next the nakani brought forward the deceased chief's dishes to be filled with food, which was then carried to the fireplace and ladled onto the fire. A ladleful was also poured into the fire for each deceased member of the clan who had died in recent years, while his or her name was called, followed by the phrase "for him" or "for her." The dishes were then placed before the chief's widow, signifying that the nakani had eaten with the chief while he was alive. Finally the guests were served.

After everyone had eaten, the people were again given tobacco and pipes to smoke. Out of respect for the dead, none of the Grizzly Bear people spoke. But the head Frog clan chief, Qalaktc of Gagan Hit (Sun House), addressed the mourning hosts.

"Yes, our friends," he said to them, "we remember you are in mourning. We are not the ones smoking this tobacco for which you have invited us, but rather these long dead uncles and aunts. Their spirits smoke along with us, just as they have partaken of the funeral feast with us." The grieving ones nodded in agreement with these words.

"Do not mourn, my friends," Qalaktc went on. "Your old chief is not dead. All his uncles have come out to greet him and are shaking hands with him. We can feel them in the room." Again the people of both clans nodded agreement and turned slightly from side to side as if greeting the spirits. The reception of the deceased chief by the illustrious **17** dead brought comfort to the Grizzly Bear people, who also took great pride that this welcome had been witnessed by their honored guests. Chief Qalaktc continued his speech, now giving a history of the Frog clan and its origins at the Nass, the same place that Raven first acquired light for mankind.

Members of all the clans knew the Raven story well—it was one of their most cherished tales.

"Your clan like ours came originally from the South in the region of the Nass, where Raven originated," he began.

■ ■ ■

In the beginning of things a being called Nascakiyel, Raven-at-the-Head-of-the-Nass, lived in a house at the head of the Nass River. Though no one had ever seen Nascakiyel, all regarded him as the creator of the world. Heron was the first being created by Nascakiyel and then Raven, whose mother on Heron's advice became impregnated by a hot stone to ensure that her child would be exceptionally hardy and not die young, like her previous children.

Both Heron and Raven were Nascakiyel's servants, but Nascakiyel came to regard Raven more highly and, after creating other beings, made him ruler of the world. When Raven was fully grown and had started his travels around the world, he noticed how hard it was for creatures to live in darkness and decided to do something about it.

Nascakiyel jealously guarded the sun, moon, and stars in his house, admitting no outsider. To get into Nascakiyel's house, Raven turned himself into a hemlock needle and floated in the drinking water of Nascakiyel's daughter, who after swallowing the needle became pregnant and gave birth to Raven. With his usual cleverness, he eventually wheedled the sun, moon, and stars from his grandfather and let them fly up into the sky.

When Raven returned to the house of Nascakiyel many years later, he saw the box that had formerly held the sun, stars, and moon still tied to the rafters. He was surprised to see his mother imprisoned in it and resolved to free her. First he went out with his bow and arrow and shot a whale, which he left to drift on the water. As the tide floated it onto the beach each day, Raven looked over the seabirds sitting on it. Finally he shot a cax and another large, pretty, white bird with a bill like copper.

Next Raven returned to Nascakiyel's house, took down the box that held his mother, and liberated the flickers she kept under her arms. Nascakiyel was heartbroken at having lost all his pretty things. When he learned that Raven was responsible for his loss, he summoned him.

"Go and fell that tree standing over there," he ordered, ordaining the tree to fall on Raven and kill him. But the tree did not injure Raven, who was born of rock. The following day Nascakiyel called Raven to him again.

"Go and clean that canoe," he ordered, pointing to a newly made canoe that had not yet had its sides widened by steaming. As Raven was cleaning it, the canoe closed in upon him. But the powerful Raven extended the sides again and broke the canoe into kindling.

Finally Nascakiyel sent for Raven a third time, put him in a large copper kettle of hot water, and placed it over the fire. But Raven changed himself into a rock and once more escaped death.

Now Nascakiyel became enraged at all the creatures of the earth and shouted, "Let rain pour down all over the world, and let everyone die of starvation!"

19

As the waters rose, the people and all other creatures were unable to find food and began to starve. When the rising waters dashed their canoes to bits on the rocks and broke up their houses, the people started to climb the mountains to escape. Raven was in Nascakiyel's house with his mother at this time, and as the waters covered the floor, they got up on the lowest retaining timber. As the water continued to rise, Raven and his mother continued to climb until they had reached the eighth and highest timber.

When Raven realized that the house would fill with water, he gave his mother the skin of the cax he had shot earlier. "Put this on quickly," he told her.

Then Raven put on the skin of the white bird with the copper bill. The cax, a great diver, floated with his mother on the surface of the water. But Raven as the white bird flew up to the highest cloud in the sky and clung to it with his beak. He hung there for several days until the white bird's copper bill pulled out, and Raven fell onto some floating kelp. He flew off, discarding his disguise, and noticed the water had receded just halfway down the mountains.

Raven then descended to the ocean floor, using a huge stick as a ladder. There he forced Tide Woman to lower the tides, making the flood recede from the land and then go still lower, so that many salmon, whales, seals, and other sea creatures lay stranded on the sand bars where the people who had survived could get them. They gathered enough food from that very low tide to supply them for a long time after the water returned once more to its normal level.

Raven did many other things for people and other creatures of the world. To make the rivers and streams he stole water from Petrel's carefully guarded spring. He put fire into rocks for mankind to use and caused mountains to rise out of the sea. He gave many creatures their roles: robins would make people happy; snipes would go in flocks; otters would live on water as well as land, with their homes by breezy points, where they could save people lost at sea.

■ ■ ■

"Because he has done so much for mankind, Raven is held in high regard by all clans," said Qalaktc, finishing his speech. When Qalaktc was seated again, the nakani began to hand out gifts to the Frog people who had prepared the body and performed the funeral service. After each of the principal donors made his gift, the Frog clan chief expressed the thanks of his clan in a profuse speech. When the gifts had been distributed, all returned to their houses. The community would continue to mourn the deceased chief less formally for a year, until they reconvened at the memorial potlatch, when the chief's ashes would be ceremonially placed in his mortuary pole.

RAVEN CREATES THE TIDES

Raven came to a certain cliff and noticed that a door into it had swung open. He hid behind the point, for he knew that the old woman who lived in this cliff controlled the tide. Looking out to sea, Raven saw some kelp in the water and flew out to it. He climbed down the strands to the roots at the bottom of the ocean and came upon many sea urchins. He gathered as many as he could take back with him.

Once ashore, he proceeded to eat his catch greedily, making loud gulping noises as he did so. Hearing these slurping sounds, the woman in the cave mocked him.

"At what low tide did you get those sea urchins?" she asked, knowing it had not been low enough for anyone to find sea urchins. When Raven ignored her, she repeated her question over and over.

"Keep quiet, you blathering old woman, or I will stick you with these sea urchin shells!" But the woman kept up her taunts. Angered, Raven flew into the cave, knocked her over, and began to prick her buttocks with the spiny shells.

"Stop, Raven, stop, or the tide will go down." This is what Raven wanted. He asked Mink to tell him when the tide got low. When it had finally uncovered everything on the beaches, Raven addressed the old woman.

"Will you let the tide rise and fall regularly through the months and years?" When she agreed, Raven stopped tormenting her. Since that time, the tide rises and falls regularly. And the sea urchin has become the mink's food.

PREPARATIONS

During the year that followed the cremation and smoking feast, the entire village prepared for the anniversary memorial potlatch. Earlier in the fall and summer, the dead chief's house, Hit Len or Big House, had kept people busy acquiring and preserving food for the banquet and gathering and making gifts—carved dishes and boxes, woven baskets, jewelry. Although the official invitations would not go out until a few weeks before the potlatch, word had been passed to all the clans involved of the time set for the ceremony and their roles in it. All the local

Grizzly houses would assist the Big House people as hosts. All the other clans in the village were invited. Honored guests would be the Frog clan people of the deceased chief's wife who had performed the funeral ceremonies. Frog people from the Frog clan village would also be invited to join the local Frog clan as guests. The Dog Salmon people of the present chief's wife, who had been asked to build the potlatch house, would be invited to dance against the Frog people.

The lively memorial potlatch would have joyful songs, dancing, and even games. Guest clans competed against each other in these events. Competition was a vital element of the potlatch. Storytellers, singers, and dancers strove to outdo one another, as the potlatch hosts strove to exceed previous hosts in the sumptuousness of the feast and the value and elegance of the gifts.

A lavish memorial potlatch raised the prestige of the honored dead chief, as well as the living members of his clan, allowing the latter to act as benefactors, dispensing largesse from their great store of wealth. For only a very wealthy chief could afford to give a large potlatch and thus be entitled to add a ring to his hat, thereby improving his chances of eventually becoming a head chief. The ringed hat, carved from wood or woven from spruce and painted with the clan crest, was worn on ceremonial occasions by the owner. The ring was a duplication of the crown, carved or woven directly above it and extending it into a cylinder. Three or four rings were common for a clan chief; five or six, unusual; and eight, extremely rare.

The showing of crests and telling of the clan history linked the living members with the dead, whose illustrious deeds added to clan status. But the memorial potlatch had an even greater importance. It was essential to honor deceased persons with an anniversary potlatch, or at least remember them at one. Otherwise their spirits would be condemned to wander after death instead of going to the Land of the Dead, or entering the body of a newborn heir to endow him with the dead man's personality and spirit powers.

The memorial potlatch also served to officially proclaim the dead chief's successor the head chief and bestow on him the name of a renowned ancestral chief. At that time, the new chief would also be allowed to give ancestral names to worthy nephews, generally those who had been chosen to live at his house and to be reared by him. For at puberty, male children of the chief's sisters went to live with their maternal uncles, who educated and trained them. Living with the head Grizzly Bear chief was an honor extended to those nephews being considered as his successor, a position awarded to the most deserving son of one of the chief's sisters. The prominence of the person whose name the boy received had a bearing on his prospects for becoming chief, for it was believed that the traits of that ancestor would be reincarnated in his namesake.

Not all people could afford to give even a small potlatch. So at a lavish feast, other members of the Eagle phratry were given the opportunity to tell an ancestral story and sing a song to honor their dead. In turn, these members would add gifts to those to be distributed at the potlatch.

When the time drew near to invite the guests formally, Chief Kowishte went to check on the preparations. As he went into the Big House, he could hear the singing of various groups practicing their songs and dances. He saw many groups of people at work around the fireplace, engaged in **25** preparing songs, dances, gifts, and food for the memorial potlatch. Other Eagle clans would also contribute food and gifts, especially those who wanted to sing a clan song or tell a clan story. All Eagles were included in the host groups; only Ravens were guests.

At the potlatch, individual gifts would be given to all the invited guests in accordance with their social standing. Kowishte had just come from reviewing the gift list with his adviser, weighing carefully the wealth and status of each person. Too small a gift could be construed as an insult to the one receiving it, but too large a gift could exact too great an obligation. The gift list would correspond to the guest seating list, also based on wealth and status. Acknowledging the guests' wealth and rank in these ways added to and reinforced the wealth, status, and power of the already rich and powerful clan members.

Even more important, though, were the clan potlatch gifts—blankets, slaves, and copper shields—that would be given to the Frog and Dog Salmon clan head chiefs and to chiefs of other high-ranking Frog and Dog Salmon houses. The value of each clan gift and the order of receiving it corresponded to the honorary seating of the chiefs. These gifts, which then belonged to the clan receiving them rather than to any individual, increased clan wealth, thereby raising clan status and power. The most prestigious gift to give or receive was the copper, a shieldlike rectangle about three feet long and a foot wide, its upper third fanning out to an extra six inches at the top. Coppers, decorated with shield designs, were highly prized, worth five slaves in exchange. Slaves, captured from distant unfamiliar tribes and forced to do household tasks no matter how high their positions in their own societies, were considered property but were freed upon certain occasions.

The wealthy Grizzly Bear people already possessed the greatest number of clan gifts, which they had acquired over the years in return for gifts they themselves had awarded at earlier potlatches or had gained as booty in wars against other clans.

Kowishte approached a group of men, women, and children practicing songs and dances. "We will need a new song to greet our Frog clan guests," he said to the leader. "Have you composed one yet?"

Gutao, chief of Tatuk Hit (Cliff House), who sang in a strong bass voice and danced well, was the Grizzly Bear song and dance leader. Upon election to this position, he received the carved paddle, the leader's official baton.

"It will come," Gutao answered the chief. "It is not a man's own will, but the way Raven made people that brings forth a new song when people are called together."

The Grizzly Bear people would sing the special old potlatch songs, of course, composed at the time of the Flood and recording those sad events. Some told of finding bodies when the flood-waters receded; others of the parting of the clans at that time. The clan valued these older, solemn songs and sang them only at large traditional feasts honoring ancestors, where they were believed to give the people special strength. After these solemn songs would come the more modern ones that marked certain events, such as the death or other harrowing experience of a close relative. In addition to rehearsing the songs and dances, both the guests and the hosts had to refurbish their ceremonial garments and make new ones, especially for the children. They would also repair or replace furs and carvings for headpieces.

As Kowishte went to see what preparations the women **27**

were making, he heard his eldest aunt issuing orders to the younger women of the house.

"I'll repair this ermine streamer that has worked loose on the chief's headdress," she said to the wife of one of her sons. "Then you can oil and polish the frontlet." The frontlet, a delicately carved and highly polished wooden square attached to a headband of animal hide, was worn over the forehead, while the ermine attached opposite it hung in layers down the back. This particular frontlet, with an ornately carved eagle, had been the present of a nephew.

"We will also need new sea lion whiskers for the head-band," she directed another young woman. The whiskers would be inserted to stand upright around the rim of the headdress. "Smooth the wrinkles from the chief's dancing shirt and hang it out to air," she ordered a third, handing her a leather garment painted with the clan grizzly bear. Kowishte admired his aunt's efficiency. But of course, he realized, this was the same aunt who had exacted a generous dowry from his in-laws when she had gone with his uncle to arrange for Kowishte's marriage.

"The Chilkat blanket should also be put out," the aunt added, watching the women open it up to hang it outside. Kowishte too regarded the blanket thoughtfully. It had been a gift from the Chilkats of Klukwan, who made them from wool of mountain-goat hides that they got by trading with the Athapaskans of the Interior. Only the very wealthy could make or own one of these valuable blankets, and it was a great privilege to wear one.

Kowishte felt a surge of pride as he gazed at this fine blanket that he would soon wear. Given originally in recognition of the Grizzly Bear clan's social and political status, it had been worn by many previous chiefs. He marveled at the intricacy with which the killer whale design had been woven into the blanket, and understood why the weavers had needed a year to finish it.

First the men had to make the pattern, a killer whale design painted on a wooden pattern board. The men also provided mountain-goat hides for the wool, but the women gathered cedar bark, worked the yarn, and wove the blanket.

The goat wool was removed from the hide by wetting and rolling it, then pushing the wool off with the thumb and fingers. It was then rolled between the palm and thigh to make the thread—two strands rolled together for the weft yarn, and two strands rolled with a strip of cedar bark for the warp.

The wool's natural color was kept for the warp, but weft yarns were dyed in traditional colors. Yellow came from the wolf-moss lichen, while dark brown was made by boiling wool in urine and hemlock bark. A greenish blue was made by first boiling the wool in copper and urine, then in wolf moss.

The men made the warp-weighted loom of two standing poles and a cross bar. From the bar hung the warp threads, their long ends tied into bundles weighted with stones to give the needed tension. The women sat or kneeled in front of the loom, weaving entirely with their fingers, twining or twisting two or more wefts around a single warp of yarn. They bordered the finished blanket with braid and fringed it with additional warp yarn.

As Kowishte moved farther along in the house, he passed men carving food dishes from cedar and inlaying the edges with dentalia or abalone. Others were making small carvings of animals for art objects or jewelry. These items could be used as individual potlatch gifts. Finally the chief came to his grandmother, who was weaving a basket from spruce roots that had been prepared earlier.

"Well, if it's not the honored guest!" she said to him. "Are you on an inspection tour?" The new chief smiled.

"Hello, Grandmother," he answered. "It's good to see everybody so busy. Everything seems to be moving right along. It is about time to send out the nakani."

Kowishte was very fond of this older woman with whom he had spent so much time as a youngster, listening to her stories of the clan history and learning from her the clan traditions and customs. It was the grandmother's place to pass on the clan culture to the children, while the mother's eldest brother and sister saw to their training in work skills. Even here, working with the younger women, his aunts and sisters, she was passing on skills and culture.

The women were cutting strips from additional roots, which had been soaked to soften them, roots that the women had dug and gathered from the base of spruce trees in the spring. Before the sap could dry and harden them, the women had stripped the bark from the roots and coiled and stored them to cure.

The chief watched as the women split the now-softened roots lengthwise into narrow strips. They separated those with a brown luster, taken from the outside of the roots and used for the weft, from the lighter ones from the inside root, which were used for the warp. The women started the split with a mussel-shell knife and then, holding the root with their front teeth, continued splitting it with the nails of their right-hand thumb and forefinger.

His grandmother was using the "close-together-work" weave on her basket, making it watertight. She had done the base and lower section in the natural tan of the root but was now weaving an intricate design in black into the upper part. This work called for wrapping dyed grasses around the weft so the pattern showed only on the outside of the basket. The grasses and thin threads of roots made the weave very fine.

As the chief left the weavers, he met his nephew Galge with some of his cousins. The boys, who had just come from their daily ritual of exercise and bathing in cold water, were on their way to practice with the dancers.

Each day Galge, who was being groomed for house chief, sat a little longer in the icy water and pushed himself a little harder in exercising. When the time came to replace the present clan chief, a council made up of the Grizzly Bear chief's brothers and sisters would decide which nephew of the chief would be best suited to be his successor.

Once Galge had proved himself as a house chief, he would be high on the list of prospects for clan chief, since his family enjoyed great wealth and the highest social status. Galge himself had followed clan traditions and customs and had shown leadership ability as well as hunting and fishing skills. Eventually he would be married to one of the new chief's daughters, a Dog Salmon Raven like her mother, a match that would further strengthen the financial position and raise the social status of both prominent clans.

The young men left to get their headbands and blankets from the storeroom and joined the dancers. In these dances, the men made most of the dance movements, which were very concentrated. When portraying a halibut, they imitated a halibut's movements; when portraying a bear, only a bear's. The children aped the men's movements, but the women merely stood and swayed. Women participated actively only when there was a special part for them.

Finally Kowishte went into the storage areas to inspect the huge supplies of food that had been laid up for serving at the banquet or giving as gifts. All the other Eagle houses in the village would also donate food, since enormous amounts would be needed.

The Grizzly Bear camp was not the only one busy preparing. The Frog people were also checking their dance costumes and masks and practicing songs and dances. But the most pressing activity for those from other villages was refurbishing travel canoes for the journey. The voyaging or "war" canoes, from thirty-five to sixty-five feet long and six to eight feet wide, could carry fifty to sixty people with baggage and gear, about a five-ton capacity. They had long, projecting prows and high, spur-shaped sterns, flaring gunwales, and gracefully curving cross-sections.

These large canoes were used for longer journeys involving several families, whereas the fifteen-passenger, two-ton family canoes took the people out to fish camps. Smaller still were the hunting and fishing dugouts, which carried only two to three people but were light and portable.

Besides making the canoes more seaworthy, the prows and sterns provided a place to display clan and tribal crests. Artists were busy now repainting these intricate designs, each using slight variations according to his skill and talents. The tribal figure of Raven and the clan Frog crest appeared on all the boats, interspersed with stylized representations of such house figures as sea lions, geese, and owls.

For the intricate design of the paintings the artists used carefully crafted brushes, which were generally made from human hair and had wooden handles carved in various totemic designs. Figures on the canoes were outlined in

black and filled in mainly with red; yellow and green or

blue-green were used less frequently. The reds were made from iron ochres, the greens and blue-greens from copper, the yellow from wolf-moss lichen, and the black from lignite or charcoal. The decorated boats lining the sandy beach were magnificent from every view. Similar motifs were carved on the yellow cedar paddles, which were kept indoors until needed.

Carved dancing sticks and woven hats, some with three or four potlatch rings, were brought out. The head chief would wear his Chilkat blanket and carry his power-giving staff, while the other dancers would be attired less elaborately in blue woven blankets trimmed in red, the clan crest depicted in button designs on the back. Some Frog people were preparing headbands, while others cleaned and mended wooden or woven hats painted with clan figures. The boys' dance tunics—skins painted with clan crests and fringed with puffin beaks—were made ready. Cloth capes bordered with buttons and decorated with beaded crests and flowers would be worn by the girls over cloth skirts.

The local Dog Salmon Ravens were also working on their serious songs and dances for the potlatch, and the leader was taking the same meticulous care as the Frog clan and Grizzly Bear leaders to have everything perfect. In addition to the many practices, leaders fasted, slept apart from their wives, and took medicines to help them perform well.

The Dog Salmon people also prepared their lighter songs and dances for the competition with the Frog people after the distribution of gifts, and like them spent many hours refurbishing their costumes and paraphernalia. The deceased chief would be memorialized with full ceremonial splendor.

RAVEN AND THE FLOOD

*S*ome time after having given the old woman beneath the earth charge of the rising and falling of the tides, Raven became curious about what was under the ocean. He had Tide Woman raise the tides off the floor of the ocean so that he could go about down there beneath the sea and see for himself.

But the rising of the tide to such great heights presented a problem for the other creatures on earth. Their homes were being flooded. Since the tide rose slowly, some of the people had time to load their canoes and get into them. But when the tide had lifted them close to the mountaintops, they could see bears there. Some bears swam out to them, but the dogs frightened them away.

Those who were able to land proceeded to wall off the mountaintops with rocks to keep out harmful creatures. They could see trees uprooted by the rush of the waters and devilfish that had been swept up onto the mountains.

Eventually the flood subsided and the people went back down with it. But the trees were all gone and, having no firewood, the people died from the cold. Raven changed the dead people and creatures into stone and then created new people from leaves. Those who promised not to hurt anyone he allowed to grow, but the others he rooted out. Then he addressed the people.

"When the tide goes out, your food will be on the shore; when it comes in, your food will be in the woods."

THE INVITATION

About two weeks before the anniversary potlatch, Chief Kowishte got ready to send the nakani to issue the formal invitations. Since the cremation ceremony the year before, the chief had been preparing for the potlatch by bathing ritually before dawn, eating sparingly, and sleeping apart from his wife. He would now have to undertake a total fast for several days before the potlatch.

Chief Kowishte sent for two of his renowned uncles, the two eldest brothers of the deceased chief's Dog Salmon wife, both men of very high rank.

35

"You two shall be the nakani for the potlatch," he told them. "You know well the Grizzly Bear and Frog clan traditions of issuing invitations and escorting guests to the potlatch. We know you will use good judgment and tact in all the proceedings. The guests will recognize your high birth and social rank and will receive you with highest regard."

"You do us a great honor," the elder brother-in-law answered. "We shall carry out your wishes carefully."

"Go invite the Frog and Dog Salmon houses in our village first," he told them. "Then you must go to the Frog people's main village and invite them there in the order of their social standing."

"We shall do this," the brothers-in-law of the dead chief answered. "And to avoid giving any offense, we shall consult the local Frog people about the standing of the visiting Frog clans so you can invite them in the proper order."

"We are pleased that you accept this mission for us," the chief replied. "The Dog Salmon people must also be invited to dance against the Frog clan guests."

The nakani took their leave of the chief and went to invite the guests in the village. The two brothers, chiefs of their own Dog Salmon houses and renowned for strict adherence to tradition, carried out their mission with precision and little fanfare.

They went first to the house where the head Frog clan chief lived.

"You, Chief Qalaktc of Gagan Hit (Sun House), and all your people are invited to the Grizzly Bear chief's anniversary potlatch." When the chief accepted, they went to stand before each of the other Frog clan houses, calling out, "You Frog people are invited." Then they proceeded to the Dog Salmon Til Hit (Dog Salmon House), and standing before it called the house chief by name. "You, Chief Tanaxk of Til Hit, and all of your house are invited." The chief accepted readily.

"The Dog Salmon are also asked to dance against the Frog clan guests," the nakani informed him.

"The Dog Salmon shall be honored to perform," replied the chief. The nakani then continued their rounds to the other Dog Salmon houses in the village, standing before each to invite the people.

In the meantime other members of the nakani's houses were getting the canoe ready for the trip to the Frog clan village. Because the journey would take several days, they loaded the boat with enough provisions to make the trip without having to stop along the way to hunt or fish.

The nakani and their attendants set out by heading north through the narrows between the islands, skillfully avoiding boulders and sandbars in the shallow, eddying waters. When it grew dark, they beached the canoe to spend the night.

Setting off again the next morning, they encountered low fog, which became thicker as they paddled by the mouth of the bay where the kushtakas were believed to reside. Keeping a safe distance from its entrance, they tried to look into the bay as they went by, but the fog obscured everything. Although fearless in other matters, the nakani shared the common wary belief in kushtakas, people who had been lured by land otters into their dens and transformed into hairy creatures that were part land otter and part human being. Kushtakas, it was believed, "saved" people lost at sea or in the woods, approaching them in the human form of their relatives, then luring them into their realm. These creatures were held responsible for other **37** kinds of mischief, too, and coming into contact with one was believed to cause insanity.

After another evening on the beach, the nakani set out for the strait, where they met spouting whales humping their long backs through the water and sending their huge tails into the air. Porpoise cavorted alongside the boat, and salmon jumped in the waters ahead as brisk southeast winds helped push the canoe along at a good speed. That night they stopped at a popular hot springs and bathed in the healing waters of the pools formed by the springs.

The water was smoother the next morning in the inner channel until they got to the shallows, where currents in the eddying tidal pools sent the boat skittering in many directions. But the seasoned boatmen had no trouble controlling their canoe, and after another day of travel they arrived at nightfall at the Frog clan village. There they camped on the beach rather than present themselves to the chief unannounced.

On their way to the chief's house the next morning, they met some of the people to be invited and greeted them.

"We come to invite the Frog clan to a Grizzly Bear potlatch in our village," the nakani told them, and they were escorted to the Chief Qoxkan of Tina Hit (Copper Plate House). The nakani stood before the house and called in loud, clear voices.

"You, Chief Qoxkan of Tina Hit, and all the Frog clan Ravens are invited to a potlatch of the Grizzly Bear Eagles at our village." Chief Qoxkan appeared at the door and came out to receive the greeting.

"The Frog people are honored to accept the Grizzly Bear invitation," the chief replied. Though they did not expect a refusal of the invitation—a grave insult that could lead to war—the nakani were somewhat surprised at the speed with which it was accepted. For sometimes, in a show of power and independence, a chief might give an ambiguous answer, requiring the nakani to return to issue the invitation. More often though, to avoid the appearance of being eager, the chief merely pretended to ignore the invitation and would talk of other things, letting the nakani know that he was a man to contend with, a man of dignity and high position.

When the Frog clan chief had finished his acceptance speech, he invited the men to come back to have dinner with him after the other invitations had been extended. Then the nakani continued their mission to the other Frog clan houses, inviting the members to the potlatch. At each stop they were received warmly and invited for refreshment and a visit. All were eager for news of the powerful Grizzly clan. Then the nakani went to issue invitations to the Dog Salmon people in the same village, and finally gave a courtesy invitation to the Grizzly Bear people, who would attend as part of the host group rather than as guests.

During their stay in the Frog people's village, the nakani spent the night with relatives and were invited to other houses for dinner, while the invited guests made last-minute preparations to leave. After each dinner there was much visiting and telling of stories until the embers burned low in the fireplace.

"How was your trip?" one of their hosts asked.

"Not bad. The water was a little rough in the strait, but easy going otherwise," one nakani answered.

"The fog was so thick in the bays we could not even see the water," the other said.

"Like at Foggy Bay when the loon led the Kats House

people out," an older man said. "The people were camping there and needed to go back to their village, but it was so foggy they could not find their way out of the bay. The only sound was the warbling of a loon. They followed the plaintive sound until they came upon the bird in the water ahead of them. As they paddled toward it, the loon kept swimming. The people followed it in their canoes, hoping it would lead them back to the shore. But as they went along, the fog became lighter and they could see that the loon had led them to the mouth of the bay."

"You have not told us that story before, Grandfather," said one of the children, who had been listening wide-eyed.

"It belongs to the Kats House, who have had the loon as their crest since that time," the old man answered. "Only they can tell the story at potlatches or large gatherings."

"Since it was also quite foggy in the channel in the bay where the kushtakas are," the nakani continued, "we tried to keep a middle course to avoid hitting rocks near the beaches. And of course, we kept our distance from the mouth of the bay."

"So you didn't meet any kushtakas?" joked one of the listeners, and the others laughed.

"Shamans are the only ones who can deal with land otters," said one of the other men. "They go after them for their tongues. That's how shamans get their spirit powers and can help people resist kushtakas."

"The first shaman to get land otter power was a Frog clan man named Kaka," said a Frog clan elder. "But he didn't get his power by cutting the land otter's tongue. The Land Otter chief gave it to him."

This story was the property of the Frog people and well known, so the old man told them a short version.

■ ■ ■

Kaka was captured by the Land Otters through the treachery of his wife, who had secretly strung a land-otter sinew through the earring hole in her husband's ear. The land-otter influence contained in the sinew caused Kaka, who was ordinarily an outstanding boatman, to lose his way when he was out fishing, and he fell into the hands of the Land Otter People. Though he refused their advances at first, he finally went with them to avoid dying at sea. But when after two years they were still unable to gain control of his mind, they sent him back with the gift of their power. Kaka became a shaman, the first man to possess the powerful Land Otter spirit.

Kaka described the Land Otter People as long, thin creatures that looked like land otters except for distorted human faces and arms that grew out of their chests. He also told his people about land otter power, which he used whenever his clan needed his help as a shaman.

■ ■ ■

"Raven first gave the land otter the power to 'save' people lost in the woods or at sea and turn them into kushtakas when he gave the animals their roles," an old woman explained to the children when the elder had finished speaking. "Children especially have to be careful not to stray too far into the woods or near the water's edge or kushtakas might find you and take you to their dens. Kushtakas appear as relatives and invite little children into their boats or kidnap them in the woods. If you bathe in the icy water daily and follow ritual practices, you will get the strength of mind and body to resist kushtakas."

After two days of feasting and listening to stories, the nakani were rested, and the Frog people were ready to start **41** on the journey. On the third morning, the nakani rose early to escort the guests to the Grizzly Bear village and the potlatch.

The guests too were up early to load their large canoes with last-minute provisions and baggage. Each canoe would take about thirty people and carried supplies and food enough for the four or five days it would take these heavily laden boats to make the trip. Food for the journey home would be supplied by the Grizzly Bear hosts. And of course the guests would also be bringing back the blankets, copper shields, and carved boxes they received as gifts. Because of the long distance between the two villages, the two communities did not visit often. This trip would allow them to see relatives and friends and to exchange news. It would also offer an opportunity to arrange for trading between the two groups in the spring.

When the boats were readied, the travelers pushed off from shore. Heading out of the bay, the colorfully painted long boats were an impressive sight. Reds, greens, and blacks gleamed on the bows and sterns of the cedar hulls that rose and fell on the choppy waters. The skin capes and woven hats of their occupants whipped in the wind. The men paddled at first to set the course and to manage the canoes in the rough seas around the point as they headed into less protected outside waters. It was a clear day and the snow-topped volcanic mountain loomed on the island to the west. Again the nakani, this time with others in their care, camped each night on the beach.

Once the flotilla reached the quieter channels, women and children were given a turn to paddle the canoes. But in the shallows the men again took control to keep the large canoes from being thrown by swirling eddies onto the rocks.

For the most part, however, the strait was calm, and when they reached the southeast side of the island, the nakani took their guests into the hot springs for the night, beaching the array of painted boats. Families set up camp and took turns bathing in the hot-spring pools. Again the travelers left early in the morning to take advantage of the calmer waters before the wind came up.

RAVEN'S CREATIONS

Once, on his continuing journey through the world, Raven camped near a stream and saw a broad-tailed fish.

"My uncle's son, come ashore here," he called to the fish. "Once when we were in our uncle's canoe, we fell into the water. So come in close." As the fish came near him, the voracious Raven grabbed its tail, intending to eat the fish. But the tail slipped through his fingers. Raven grabbed again, but again it slipped away. Each time Raven grabbed the fish's tail, it became slimmer until eventually it took its present slender form. Raven gave up and named the fish Sculpin.

On his next stop Raven gathered many small birds together and sent them in search of fresh water. Then he set about creating a creek and put a woman at its head to attract the salmon. To this day salmon runs go upstream every year to see Woman-at-the-Head-of-the-Creek.

From there Raven went into the woods, where he saw a small animal scurrying away from a bear. "This little creature needs protection," he thought. He began carving slim pieces of bark from the yellow cedar to serve as quills. These he arranged up and down the animal's back and sides to make him prickly—and unappetizing to any animal.

"When anyone threatens you," he told the newly created porcupine, "spread your tail and throw your quills like darts. Then nobody can get near enough to harm you. New quills will grow in place of those you have shed."

HOUSE BUILDING

A year after the tobacco and cremation ceremony for the deceased head chief of the Grizzly Bear clan, the elaborate memorial potlatch was held. The first four days of this joyous anniversary potlatch would be devoted to entertaining guests at feasts that included singing and dancing in the houses of various Grizzly Bear chiefs. Then came a day of more serious events, when members of the host clan sang their ancestral songs and told the clan stories that traced their lineage and their claim to certain rights and properties before guests whose presence affirmed these claims. In the final three days, the guests competed with songs and dances to thank their hosts for honoring them with a feast and gifts.

Before the memorial potlatch could be given, a mortuary pole to hold the ashes of the dead chief needed to be carved, and a new house had to be built for the ceremonies and to serve afterward as the residence of the new chief. Shortly after the smoking feast, men of the Dog Salmon clan, along with Chief Kowishte and his advisers, had gone to select a suitable red cedar tree for the pole. When Kowishte gave his approval of the tree, the Dog Salmon men felled it, cut it to the desired length, and trimmed and peeled away the bark. Then they skidded it into the water, towed it to the village, and beached it where it would be prepared for carving.

The carver and his helpers set to shaping the log with their adzes and marked off the areas to be carved. This pole would depict only the footprints of the Grizzly Bear figure that was to be set on the top of the raised pole (commemorating the Bear's leading the people in the climb to the mountaintop at the time of the Flood). But it would take many working hours for the carver to chisel out the prints and then sculpt them with his various curved knives. The bear at the top, carved from a smaller nearby tree and treated in the same way as the post log, had to be shaped with a broadaxe before the adze was used. Then the carver made a pattern and lay it over the shaped wood to trace it. He drew in by hand details of the haunches and forepaws and the eyes, ears, and mouth. Again he used chisels and knives to do the carving.

When he had finished the first phase of both parts of the pole, the carver had to go over them with a small adze rounded at the edge to create a smooth, evenly patterned surface. Afterward he would paint the bear and the footprints with black paint made from lignite. The bear would be affixed to the log by means of a heavy wooden pin, or tenon, inserted into each.

Since the house required less time to complete, it was commissioned much later. One day two months short of the one-year anniversary of the cremation ceremony, the Grizzly Bear chief, Kowishte, who still kept his face darkened in memory of his deceased predecessor, got up before daybreak and called for Kitlen of Kut Hit (Box House), his uncle and the dead chief's brother.

"Today I shall call upon the Dog Salmon people, my wife's clan, to build the potlatch house," Kowishte said.

"First we must call on our own people to consult with them," Kitlen, an authority on ceremonial protocol, replied. "We must go to each house to make an announcement." So they went out and stood before the first house. Kowishte needed no prompting to call out to the sleepers inside.

"See how I drift out with the tide!" he cried, which meant "I need your help." In this way he called Grizzly Bear people together to ask their opinions and advice. Those who heard knew that Kowishte was alluding to his intention of building the house and raising a pole, the highest honors paid to a deceased person. Such an undertaking also attested to the wealth and status of the clan.

"We honor our chief's call," the chief of each house replied.

"Tomorrow morning before daybreak," Kowishte announced. The following morning the members of the Grizzly Bear houses met and discussed plans for building the new house. From that time until the house was completed, **47**

Kowishte ate sparingly and slept apart from his wife so that all would go smoothly without injury to anyone. Though the Dog Salmon clan of the chief's wife did the actual labor, Kowishte oversaw the project and was responsible for its outcome.

A few days later the Grizzly Bear chief went out again before daybreak, this time to the house of the highest chief of the Dog Salmon clan, where he sang out, "I run into the bosom of your mother's memorial pole." He referred to the pole that the Dog Salmon chief had erected upon his mother's death. Then as he left, Kowishte sang the song used by his own ancestor who had built the house he intended to rebuild. The Grizzly Bear chief visited all the Dog Salmon houses and, standing before each one, sang out a similar refrain, mentioning a pole or house erected by the members of that house. The message was clear to the Dog Salmon people, who began to gather around Kowishte.

"The new Grizzly Bear chief would like us to build the house for his deceased uncle's anniversary potlatch," announced the head Dog Salmon chief, Tanaxk of Til Hit. It was considered an honor to be asked to perform such a task, and the payment received would further enrich the Dog Salmon clan, to which Kowishte's wife and children belonged. The Dog Salmon people agreed to build the house. Kowishte had Kitlen assign tasks to the Dog Salmon men, and then the two Grizzly Bear chiefs went with them into the woods. "You are to cut that tree," Kowishte instructed the Dog Salmon men, pointing to a red cedar he and his advisers had selected previously for planks or posts. The men assigned to procure logs set about cutting with their axes other trees the Grizzly Bear chief pointed out.

48   Within a few days the logs were ready, and the Dog

Salmon people floated them to the site of the new house. There they were met by Kowishte, who greeted them and invited them into his house to eat. When the meal was finished, one of the Dog Salmon chiefs spoke at length about various past chiefs of his clan and finished by saying that the deceased Grizzly Bear chief was now among them.

Kitlen then answered with a speech about the deceased chief, in whose honor the house was being built. Then he turned toward Kowishte. "Get up now," he commanded. "Your wife's clansmen are getting tired." At this signal Kowishte rose and the guests left for home.

The following day the logs were rolled up onto the beach, and the Dog Salmon leaders appointed different groups of their clansmen to strip the bark and trim and adze them. Others were directed to dig the post holes, place the posts, and put the beams in position next to them. A post was set at each of the four corners of the house to support the plate beam. A post was then set in the center of each side wall, and two others were placed at each gable end to support the three rafters. During the several weeks it took to finish all this work, the Dog Salmon men were fed each night by their host.

When the poles were set, all the Dog Salmon people helped hoist the beams onto the posts with skids and ropes. To serve as a skid, a sturdy plank was placed against the first post, which was braced on the opposite side. The beam log was manipulated on skids to lie on the ground along the length of the house. Ropes of spruce root or twisted cedar bark were tied around one end of the log, pulled up over the top of the post, and wrapped around a tree trunk. Next, everyone pulled on the ropes to raise the end of the log to the top of the post. Men hurried to place forked sticks under the raised part of the log to help support its weight. They shifted these supports toward the log's center as its end was pulled high enough to place on its post. This process was repeated at the other end of the house frame: all the other beams were raised in the same way. When raised, the house frame was complete and the ceremony of "feeding the house" took place.

While the nakani went from house to house to invite the guests to this celebration, a fire was built in the center of the new structure. The assembled visitors took hold of a rope and stood around the sides and head of the house, forming an outline of its perimeter. Next, while the Grizzly Bear people sang eight ancestral songs, the nakani poured a ladle of grease first on the fire, then on each of the junctures of the posts and the beams at the house corners. These songs and rituals ensured that the spirits of their ancestors would dwell in the house and signified that the leadership traits of previous chiefs would continue to guide the new one in his governance of the Grizzly Bear clan. Honoring the illustrious dead also reminded all present of the high status and power of the hosts, which reflected also to some extent on the builders, since the two clans were united by marriage. After the new house was nourished in this way, thus hallowed with the presence of ancestral spirits, the hosts invited their guests to join in a feast and receive gifts for their work so far.

The wood for the walls and planks was then prepared and put in place, an undertaking of several more weeks. The walls were enclosed with rough split planks placed vertically. The roof consisted of two or three courses of shorter boards laid across the frame and overlapped, like shingles. A square opening in the center, a smokehole, had a movable flap that could be adjusted to keep out rain. The unsealed space between the roof and the walls allowed air to circulate in the house. An oval door was cut in the center of the front wall.

When the house was finished, the host again went through the ritual of asking his clansmen for help and inviting the guests. Then the feast to celebrate the completion of the house began. After everyone had eaten, the host group sang songs involving Grizzly Bear clan lineage and history. Then Chief Tanaxk of Til Hit rose to speak.

"The illustrious history of the Grizzly Bear clan is well known, Chief Kowishte. We share your pride in it. This house will be a fine testament to it. The Dog Salmon clan too have a great lineage." Then he began to tell one of the stories shared by the Raven clans of Raven's exploits in early times during his journey throughout the world.

■ ■ ■

Raven was traveling with Cormorant, and they came to a brown bear camp. As he approached the camp, Raven turned himself into a woman and won the affections of a brown bear. After they were married, the bear brought a large halibut to camp, and his "wife" asked for its stomach to prepare for dinner. When she cooked the stomach, however, she filled it with hot rocks. Then she served it to her bear husband, telling him it tasted best when swallowed whole. Cormorant tried to warn the bear, but Raven quickly plucked out the bird's tongue.

"Cormorant says the halibut is very good," Raven explained, directing Cormorant to get some water for the bear, who now appeared to have indigestion. The bear took the water readily and drank large amounts to ease his distress. But then he began to expand like a balloon, and steam came out his mouth and nostrils. Soon he fell over dead.

51

Raven chased Cormorant to the offshore rocks and proceeded to eat the halibut and the bear meat. When he had finished his huge meal, Raven took the bearskin and flew on until he came to a camp where children were trying to roast herring. He showed them how to put the herring on slender sticks and hold them over the fire. Then he went into the woods to put on the bearskin and returned to camp. When the frightened children ran off, Raven ate the cooked herring, ran into the woods to take off the bearskin, and returned to camp as himself. The children told him what had happened.

"Go on with your cooking, and if the bear returns, beat it with clubs to drive it away," he advised them, believing they would be too frightened to do this.

The children once again skewered the herring and put them over the fire. But when Raven returned in the bearskin, the children were ready for him. They attacked the "bear" with clubs and hit him so hard that Raven took off the skin, pretending it was all a joke. The children laughed and shared their fish with Raven before he set off on another adventure.

■ ■ ■

"When Raven married the bear, a Wolf phratry animal crest, he started the custom of marriage between opposite sides," Chief Tanaxk explained as he ended the story. All the listeners understood the importance of tracing clan customs to the time of Raven and the beginning of all things. Their common roots, reinforced by the custom of marriage between clans, further cemented the relationship between the Grizzly Bear and Dog Salmon people. Then Tanaxk turned to his own Dog Salmon clan.

"Our brother-in-law has been in mourning," he told

them. "Now, my clansmen, tie your belts! Let us get up and sing for him." The song leader started a song, and all the guests joined in. Then they marched out of the house and went to their homes to don their dance costumes. Returning, they danced into the hall in single file chanting one of their songs.

Suddenly the dance leader called out, "Watch! Watch what will come through the door." In leaped a special dancer, his head and face covered by a wooden headpiece carved in the image of an owl. He launched into the owl dance, and was followed by other special dancers imitating the coho, the goose, and the sea lion—all Dog Salmon crest animals—while singing the appropriate songs. One of the guest chiefs called out the names of several Grizzly Bear chiefs and addressed a speech to them, mentioning also some of the illustrious dead of his own clan and their ties with the deceased chief in whose honor the house was built.

"Thank you, my brothers-in-law, for the consolation you have offered us," the host Kowishte said to the guests. Next he addressed the deceased chief. "Now Uncle, open the door for your brothers-in-law. You have kept them bound. Now let them pass out in peace." This was a signal that the end of the mourning period was approaching. Then the Grizzly Bear people sang a song belonging to the deceased, after which the guests marched out, signifying the end of the evening's events.

IN THE WHALE'S BELLY

Taking up his travels again, Raven came upon a whale in the sea. He noticed that every time the whale came up, it opened its mouth wide. With his knife under one wing and some firewood under the other, Raven flew into the whale's open mouth. From the inside he could feast on fish and herring that the whale swallowed. Then he lit a fire inside the whale to render its fat.

Little by little he devoured the whale's organs, finally eating its heart. Then the whale died and floated to the top of the water. Raven made a wish for the whale to land on a sandy beach, which after many repetitions was granted. Some young boys shooting bows and arrows on the beach saw the large creature and heard a voice coming from inside: "I wish somebody would make a hole in my head so he can be my friend." The boys hurried to report their experience to their relatives, who came down and heard the message themselves. They cut a hole at the place from which the sound was coming and Raven flew out and into the trees.

Recognizing the creature as a whale, the people cut it up and began to render the fat for oil. As they were finishing, Raven appeared as a suave gentleman and asked if they had heard a strange sound from the whale. When the people replied that they had, he warned them that if they stayed there they could be killed. People of another village who had heard a similar sound from a dead whale had been destroyed by it. So they went off, leaving all the whale meat and oil for Raven to enjoy.

WELCOME

S everal days later the procession of brightly painted war canoes pulled into the bay of the Grizzly Bear village. According to custom, all the guests camped on the beach while the nakani hurried to the village to announce their arrival, for it would not do for the hosts to be caught unprepared for their visitors. The guests would spend the night in quarters provided by the Grizzly Bear people, who also supplied them with food and firewood.

Before leaving the beach the next morning, the dancers got ready for the greeting songs and dances. After donning their ceremonial garments, they set about painting their faces with charcoal and ochre. The dance leader of the head chief's house had darkened his upper and lower eyelids with charcoal to form a circle around each eye, with yellow rays of ochre going out from it to portray the sun, his house crest. Another dance leader used the Frog clan's goose emblem, with the head in yellow on his forehead, the neck stained blue by blueberry juice that went down the bridge of the nose, and the blue body and feet covering the base of the nose and the mouth. A third leader used just the head of the goose, with the head and bill on the nose and the wings at the sides of the face. All sprinkled their hair with down to indicate that they came in peace.

When everything was ready, the nakani led the dancers up the beach toward the village, while the rest of the guests got into their canoes again to await the Grizzly Bear welcome. As the dancers approached the Big House, Kowishte, surrounded by the villagers who had gathered near the houses on the beach, came down to greet them. His face was painted with the Killer Whale crest, a black horizontal stripe going down the side of his face and curving across his chin. His uncle, Kitlen, had jets of the killer whale's spray painted from his forehead over his eyelids and cheeks down to his chin. Both men were dressed in ceremonial regalia, as were all the Grizzly Bear people.

First came the ritual indicating that the arrivals were not intruders but guests on a peaceful mission. At first sight of their hosts, the guests broke into song and dance, the leader signaling with his decorated staff and calling out the words. In this peace song, traditionally sung upon the arrival of the guests, deep male voices in unison with women's higher pitched ones echoed sonorously as the tambourine-like drums beat the rhythms of the dance. As the guests danced, eagle down flew in airy, cottony wisps from the tops of their headpieces, where it had been nested inside the crown of seal whiskers. It floated as a gesture of peace over the heads of their hosts. On the song's final note, the Frog clan chief extended his arms in a gesture of peace.

The air was still as the Frog people returned to their canoes and pulled away from shore. Then the Grizzly Bear singers and dancers burst into their welcoming numbers, blowing eagle down on their guests through a pipe. The ceremony ended with the Grizzly Bear chief's similar spread-armed gesture of peace and welcome.

Then, in a veiled request for directions to Hit Len, the Grizzly Bear chief's house, the Frog clan song leader called out in a loud voice: "Where is the Great Bear lying?"

"You are anchoring in front of it," the Grizzly Bear chief replied, and stooped to roll up his leggings. Then he waded into the water toward the head Frog clan chief, who had taken his canoe into the water to await the formal invitation to come ashore.

"Welcome," Chief Kowishte intoned with dignity, touching first the boat of the Frog clan chief Qoxkan. "You and all of your clan are welcome." Next he went over and repeated the welcome to the Dog Salmon chief Tanaxk, who had also gone out in the canoe with his dancers to receive the formal welcome. Then Kowishte returned to shore and went up to the tribal house, leaving the nakani to escort the guests. The canoes bearing Chief Qoxkan and Chief Tanaxk were again beached, and the guests removed their ceremonial garments before going to the Grizzly Bear chief's house for the welcoming feast.

First they were led to the newly built potlatch house to   **57**

witness the raising of the mortuary pole. The Dog Salmon
men had readied the log for raising by block-and-tackle, a
method they had learned from observing the rigging of visiting sailing ships. They had anchored the block to a sturdy
tree nearby and set the ropes and guy wires in place. Many
Dog Salmon men were required to pull on the parallel
ropes to raise the pole. As the pole was slowly elevated, each
two or three feet the men would shift the support poles
until it stood upright in the hole previously dug for it.
When the pole was raised, the guests left for the chief's
house. Dog Salmon nakani stayed behind long enough to
put the bones and ashes of the deceased chief, now in a
newly carved box, in the hollow made for it in the back of
the pole.

When they had all gathered, the nakani ushered the
men into the house first. He led them to the back, the place
of honor in any clan house, since it is farthest from the front
entry, which is closest to the cold and to danger.

The two principal rival chiefs, Frog and Dog Salmon,
were placed side by side, and the lesser chiefs of each clan
next to their leaders. The nakani then directed the other
important men of each clan to the rear rows, seating them
according to status, those of highest rank closest to the
leader and the younger men toward the front. Frog clan
women guests sat toward the rear along the half of the side
wall near their clan men, and Dog Salmon women sat similarly along the other side wall near their men. Host women
stood along both side walls next to the women guests and
near the host men, who stood at the front on either side of
the door.

Song leaders found their places in front of the men of
their group, where they sat in chairs, their dance paddles

ready. These paddles or poles were of utmost importance, since the singers watched them closely to know when to pitch their voices higher or lower in their chants. The host chief stood by the door, flanked by other Grizzly Bear house chiefs. Other host men stood behind them, those of highest rank closest to the leader.

When all were seated, the Grizzly Bear chief Kowishte, clad in his Eagle Chilkat blanket, rose to welcome them.

"To the warmest place under my wings I welcome you." He chanted the traditional words, stretching out his blanket-draped arms to suggest the wings of an eagle. "To the warmest place under my feathers I welcome you." Then the nakani gave the signal for the food to be served. After the meal, guests from the other villages went to the houses of their relatives, while those with relatives in the Big House stayed there.

The next morning one of the prominent Grizzly Bear house chiefs sent out invitations to a party at his house to entertain the Frog and Dog Salmon people with feasts and dancing on the first of four days of festivities before the potlatch proper. Before the raven's call at dawn, the song leaders in the host house rose to sing the dancing songs.

"You are invited! High-class people are going to eat!" they sang as they went from house to house, inviting the Frog and Dog Salmon people and announcing the time and place of the feast to be held that evening. The guests spent most of the day getting songs, dances, and costumes ready for the party.

In the evening the guests gathered before the feast house at the appointed time. Members of each guest clan then entered the house, one after another, in their ceremonial

59

garments, dancing and singing the clan walking song as they came through the door. Once all were inside, each group did its dancing song. Then all the guests joined in the four popular songs, the *sagu*, that were common property of the clans, happy songs on light subjects and sung mainly for entertainment. During the feast, the guests sang similarly entertaining sitting-down songs, the *quin da ciyi*.

When most of the people had eaten, the dance leader of one guest clan did the ptarmigan song and dance, imitating that bird's movements. Another did the halibut dance, imitating a halibut flopping on the beach. The dancer leapt up and came down on his knees and then bent back, almost touching the floor. He continued to bend backward and forward in imitation of a fish flopping, making the feathers that were tucked into his headband fly in all directions, and ended in the kneeling position. Another Frog clan dancer, acting out a bear story, tried to catch a man in front of him with his claws. Animals imitated in these dances were from the dancers' own crests.

Finally came the feast. The host group put on the customary show of luxury, lavishing large amounts of food upon their guests—salmon, cod, and halibut, cakes made from pounded roots, seaweed and kelp dishes, all kinds of berries, and of course the ever-present dish of eulachon oil, rendered from small smeltlike fish, for dipping or pouring over food. The deceased chief's favorite foods were also served, and portions were thrown onto the fire so that his spirit could enjoy the spirit of the food.

When the feast ended, the guests danced out in the same form and manner as they had danced in, returning to the houses where they were staying. But their sleep was cut short again the next morning—they were awakened early by still another song of invitation to feast that evening. For two more nights it continued, each evening's feast more sumptuous than the night before. And each night the Dog Salmon and Frog clans held lively competitions in eating as well as in drinking great quantities of seal oil.

Competition was intense as the Dog Salmon and Frog people, wearing costumes and face paint, came onto the floor to dance against each other. The dancers leapt and flung themselves about, each group trying to outdo the other in violent movements and shouting. The nakani did their best to keep the rivalry from leading to real hostility. When serious disagreements threatened, calmer members of the host group came between the potential combatants and turned slightly to the left and right in the manner of peace hostages and showed their garments, saying, "See what I have on." These words and gestures, symbolic of peace, produced a calming effect on the riotous dancers.

RAVEN SENDS FISH TO THE STREAMS

One day Raven came to a place where he could see a house floating far out at sea, where Nascakiyel had put it for safekeeping. Raven knew this house was full of all kinds of fishes, but he did not know how to get at them. While puzzling over his dilemma, he saw a monster with a spear like the arm of a devilfish. Raven was fascinated by this weapon and agreed to marry the monster's daughter in order to obtain it.

Taking his new weapon with him, Raven paddled his canoe out to the house and sent his spear through it. He could hear all kinds of songs sung by different voices coming from the house, songs people now sing during the fishing season. When Raven threw his spear, it became very long and wrapped itself around the house so firmly that he could pull it toward his canoe. But he had to keep singing, "I think so! I think so!" a song known to all Raven people. Whenever he let up, the house would move back to the original place.

Three times it went back, but the fourth time Raven was able to pull it in far enough to beach his canoe. The door of the house opened and out came various kinds of fishes. Raven sang out to them, "Some of you go to Stikine River. Some of you go to Chilkat River," and the fishes did as he commanded. Then he sang, "Some go to the small creeks to feed the poor people." That is how fish came to the rivers and streams.

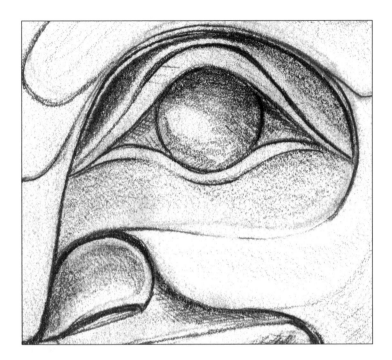

THE POTLATCH

After the four days of feasting and entertainment, the time came for the serious memorial potlatch celebration at the house built for this ceremony, when host groups mourned the deceased chief and all their dead.

The nakani ushered guests and hosts to their assigned seats, making every effort to avoid conflict among guests, treating all with equal solemnity. The nakani sat both chiefs side by side. First came the Frog clan chief Qoxkan of Tina Hit with regal stride and solemn bearing, his head high and eyes straight ahead. With equal courtesy and decorum the nakani escorted Dog Salmon chief, Tanaxh of Til Hit, to his place next to the Frog clan chief. Then members of these houses were led to the seats that their rank required.

The next-ranking Frog clan chief, Qalaktc of the local Gagan Hit, was then seated on the other side of Chief Qoxkan, and his house members after him. The remaining guest chiefs and their houses were seated with the same careful attention to rank and lineage. Finally the remaining house groups of the local village, led by their chiefs, were seated with their Raven or Eagle phratries.

Kowishte, the host chief, stood at the door, flanked on each side by nakani. Kitlen stood directly behind him, ready to prompt him with a suitable reply to a guest chief so that no insult would be inferred from the chief's answer. Kitlen had exceptional understanding of protocol and the quick-thinking, diplomatic ease necessary for this sensitive position. The rest of the Grizzly Bear men stood behind these dignitaries at the front of the house. As before, the nakani remained watchful; even in the midst of celebration, the intense competition among houses and clans could lead to hostile behavior that, becoming violent, could result in war.

The hosts, whose heritage was being celebrated in the telling of their stories, wore their most elaborate costumes. The Eagle, Grizzly Bear, and Killer Whale crests appeared in various forms on blankets and hats of the house chiefs. On display along the wall behind the guests were the many possessions of the clan: a Chilkat blanket; several button blankets depicting the crest Eagle, Grizzly Bear, Dogfish, Shark, and Killer Whale; and a large carving of the serpent-like sea monster Gonakadet. The house posts depicted the shark. Displayed in the center of the room was the preserved bearskin and head, a replica of the clan crest Bear. An antlered headdress representing the Deer of the Peace Dance ceremonies stood next to the famed Killer Whale drum acquired along with the crest, story, staff, Kit (Killer Whale) Canoe, and other related properties acquired in settlement of a war with the Tsimshian Blackfish clan.

Against the wall stood the Killer Whale staff, symbol of the authority of the head Grizzly Bear chief. Woven hats and baskets and carved hats and food dishes lay among carved animal masks and killer whale figures. Large bent-wood boxes, coppers, and carved paddles lined the walls. Galge, the chief's nephew, sat in ritual garb in the honored position among all these luxury items that attested to his family and clan wealth.

The display of wealth and the songs and dances accompanying it offered the people opportunity to affirm rights that went with these things—the rights acquired by dead ancestors by purchase or gift to stories, songs, dances, and crests as well as streams, hunting grounds, and berry patches, and sometimes even rights to the house itself. The chief would reaffirm these rights in his speeches after each of the ritual songs.

The guests wore ordinary clothes, the men in long buckskin shirts and trousers and the women in buckskin shirts, long skirts, and cloaks of woven soft cedar bark or animal fur. The children wore long buckskin shirts, some with cedar-bark cloaks over them. Some of the adults and children wore cedar-bark hats, and everyone wore moccasins. The guests would not put on their ceremonial garments until their turn came to entertain the hosts at the feasts after the distribution of gifts. Then they would appear in splendid fur-trimmed headgear, beaded moccasins, and blankets emblazoned with beaded and button-worked clan crests. A few would carry beaded octopus bags—skin purses with long beaded tendrils hanging from the bottom.

When all were seated, a shrill cry of an eagle went up to announce the arrival of the Grizzly Bear head chief. The crowd fell silent as Chief Kowishte appeared before them in his ermine headdress with the carved Eagle frontlet and his Chilkat blanket woven with the Killer Whale crest. He now carried the sacred Killer Whale staff, symbol of his authority and might.

"To the warmest place under my wings I welcome you." Stretching out his arms, Kowishte repeated to the assembled company the welcome he had given earlier to the Frog people.

"To the warmest place under my feathers I welcome you." This time, the occasion was more solemn. He spoke of his sorrow and recounted the reasons for the potlatch.

"Last year my uncle, head chief of the Grizzly Bear clan, died. After his death we mourned him for many days. Then we burned his body. Many of you were here for the funeral ceremony performed by the Frog people. Then the Dog Salmon people were called upon to carve my uncle's mortuary pole and to build this house for the anniversary potlatch. The bones of the deceased chief, gathered after the cremation and stored in the grave house, have just been placed in the newly raised mortuary pole by the Dog Salmon nakani. We are gathered today to honor the anniversary of this great chief's death."

Chief Kowishte stood awhile as if in meditation. Then he intoned the first of the eight ritual mourning songs, relating ancestral history and the arrival of the clan at the present location.

...

Hīn yîx yakᵘgwasā´x îkᴀnē´k ᴀxkā´k.

The noise of your death, my uncle, will come down through the river.

Nādadᴀ´x gᴀdjîxā´n nādāgawu´.

From the nation has fallen down the nation's drum.

...

Phrases of these verses were repeated over and over as the dancers swayed to the rhythm of the song. At a signal from the song-leader, the entire host group joined in the singing. All present united in remembering the dead and weeping for them.

The deep tones of a large box-shaped drum, its sides formed by a single bent plank of cedar sewn together at the side with sinew and painted with a killer whale in red and black, marked a mournful rhythm to the songs. On its top was carved a large dorsal fin inlaid with opercula and eight tufts of hair. On each side of the fin was carved a human figure seated on a human head, memorializing Natasee, the hero who had aided a killer whale stuck on a rock and who later, similarly marooned, was then rescued by a killer whale. The drummer had his hand thrust through an opening in the back of the drum, which he beat from the inside to produce its deep, vibrating tones.

When the song ended, Chief Kowishte came forward to address the crowd. He began with the ritual recounting of the history of the Grizzly Bear clan, which the people had heard many times before and knew by heart.

"We came originally from the south, but more recently from the Taku. A family dispute caused us to move from the Taku, and we stopped first on an island at the mouth of the Stikine. But storms forced us to move to the mainland near the river. There the Grizzly Bear people thrived under the two brothers, Koxcu and Shaddesty, until Koxcu's son insulted his uncle Shaddesty by cutting his face in an argument. In reparation to his brother, Koxcu offered twenty slaves, but Shaddesty demanded instead the Grizzly Bear dancing hat. Koxcu refused to give it up, but to keep peace, he went with his family, slaves, and all his possessions in search of a new home. After considering various sites, Koxcu spied a cluster of trees that reminded him of their old home, and the clan settled at that place, our present home. They called it Kotslitan, our name for the poplar trees that were cut down to build the houses.

"When Koxcu died, his sister's son became Grizzly Bear chief. During this time we won the right to the Killer Whale crest from the Blackfish people." The chief held forward his staff surmounted with a carved killer whale.

"The former owners of the Killer Whale crest and all the property that went with it, people with whom we had traded oil for animal skins, started the war by taking the head of Koxcu, preserved in honor in a magnificent carved box, to demand ransom for it."

Chief Kowishte, who had controlled himself thus far, began to weep at the memory of this humiliation and grief. Then he intoned another mourning song:

■ ■ ■

Help me with your believing, Grizzly Bear children. It is as if my grandfathers' house were turning over with me. Where is the person who will save me?

■ ■ ■

When the song was finished, Kowishte went on with the story of the conflict.

"Unable to tolerate this abominable insult, the Grizzly Bear people set upon the Blackfish men when they returned the next spring to trade and took several of them captive. Then our great shaman told us to prepare for war. So the following spring when the Blackfish came to rescue their people we were prepared and defeated them easily, capturing their prized Kit Canoe. To make peace the following year, our conquered enemy gave us the right to the canoe as well as the Killer Whale crest and story."

The chief then began the story of the master carver and hunter Natsilane and the Killer Whale.

■■■

Natsilane was supreme in his craft of spear-making. He fit each spear for length and weight to the man who ordered it. He used the same care in everything he did. But Natsilane, by his skill and zeal to please his wife's family, instead only antagonized his wife's brothers. On sea lion hunts, Natsilane always leaped first onto the rocks, so that when his brothers-in-law arrived, all the animals he had failed to kill had escaped into the water. Soon Natsilane's reputation as a hunter began to overshadow theirs. Envious, they plotted to get rid of him.

On their next seal-hunting trip Natsilane was again the first to leap ashore. But the brothers-in-law paddled away, leaving him there to die. Only the youngest boy cried out for them to go back.

When Natsilane realized he had been left without food and clothing, he tried to spear a sea lion, but his spearhead broke off inside it. Tired and hungry, Natsilane fell asleep. He was awakened by a man, who led him to a den of sea lions beneath the rock. There he was able to save the son of the sea lion chief from death by removing his own

69

spearhead from the animal's side. As a reward, the sea lion chief sent Natsilane home in an inflated sealskin bladder.

"Keep your thought on your home," the chief told him, and Natsilane did so, eventually arriving at a beach a few miles from his village. In secret he gathered his carving tools and returned to the beach, where he set about carving a blackfish or killer whale. His first attempt was in spruce, but when he tested it in the chain of four ponds he had made, the blackfish floated long enough to jump from the first pond to the second but then sank. A second blackfish of hemlock made it to the third pool, and a third, of red cedar, got to the fourth pond. Only the yellow-cedar blackfish jumped from pond to pond and then into the sea.

Natsilane called the blackfish to him and instructed it to find his brothers-in-law and drown them by destroying their canoe, but to save the youngest boy whom he had heard begging them to return to the rock. When this was done, Natsilane commanded the blackfish to do only good to humans in the future, making it an omen of good luck.

■ ■ ■

"That is why the Killer Whale is carved on the Grizzly Bear staff, the symbol of Grizzly Bear authority," Chief Kowishte concluded. "And that is why we have the Kit or Killer Whale canoe and use this crest for our hats and blankets and ceremonial garments."

"But older than the Killer Whale crest is the Grizzly Bear, our main crest, acquired at the time of the Flood." Then he began to relate the sacred Grizzly Bear story.

■ ■ ■

At the time of the flood the people saw the waters rising higher and higher until it covered the whole beach. They left their possessions and ran deeper into the woods to reach higher ground and escape the water rushing toward them. Soon they reached the base of a mountain.

"We will have to climb the mountain. The water keeps rising and will soon cover this ground," the chief said. He looked for a cleared place to go through the woods. As they went through the undergrowth, they came upon a bear.

Their first reaction was to pull away and start back toward the beach. Then they realized that the bear was also headed up the mountain. It seemed that he motioned to them to follow and called to them.

"Do not be afraid," they heard him say. "I have come to save you."

So they formed a line behind him. The bear knew the swiftest, most direct way to spiral up the mountain. As he plunged ahead of the people, his weight matted down the brush and made the walking faster and easier for them.

The grizzly bear stayed with the people for some time, and they were very grateful to him for saving them. But soon they were in need of food, for there was almost nothing edible on the mountain peak. So they were forced to sacrifice the bear to save themselves from starving. They used the meat sparingly so that it would last until the waters subsided. They had taken great care in skinning the bear and were able to preserve the hide with the claws and teeth and skull intact for many years after the flood. When the original hide wore out, they replaced it with the hide of another bear and continued to do so until the present.

■ ■ ■

"Because it had led them to safety and then sacrificed its life to feed them, the grizzly bear is highly respected by the Grizzly Bear people and became our main crest animal," Kowishte concluded. The chief finished by chanting the   **71** song of the legendary Grizzly Bear, which began: "Come here, you Bear, highest of all bears."

When Kowishte had finished his eight mourning songs interspersed with stories of lineage and status, he called on his nephew Galge to sing a song honoring one of his ancestors. These memorial songs were very solemn, often commemorating the mishaps and deaths that ensued as their ancestors carved out the clan history.

The Grizzly Bear chief's nephew seemed to grow in dignity and stature as he came forward in his Chilkat blanket with its all-over pattern of killer whales and his ermine headband with eagle frontlet. He began to sing a mourning song for a Frog clan bride:

■ ■ ■

This Eagle has taken his Raven bride to a good sandy beach. It is enough to make one cry. A Raven, however, always comes to amuse her.

■ ■ ■

As Galge repeated these verses over and over he took several small steps first to the right and then to the left, turning each way slightly. Grizzly Bear women swayed, moving their feet in place to the rhythm.

After Galge's song, Chief Kowishte then invited each member of the Grizzly Bear clan to sing and give a speech, introducing each by his potlatch name, his name of honor. These songs and accompanying dances were done to exhibit a crest or heirloom acquired in a particular way.

Once the singer had started the song, the rest of the clan joined in. Some were mourning songs composed for the dying or the dead in the legendary past or at least a generation ago. The words were sorrowful, and the tunes solemn with heavy, slow rhythms. Each told the story of what had happened to the singer's lost relatives and mentioned each of their names.

"It is not Raven's town I am crying about," one of the singers mourned. "It is my own grandfather's town I am crying about. Poor Dorsal-Fin-of-the-Killer-Whale-Seen will die before he reaches it."

"This is the song the Grizzly Bear Gucdutin sang when he was caught in a storm going to visit his Raven in-laws," the singer explained. "Gucdutin thought he was drowning and would not see his wife's relatives."

Singing a mourning song also required that much wealth be given away. One Grizzly Bear house chief, who had donated many large baskets and boxes to the potlatch gifts, sang a mourning song for his brother who had died in a hunting accident. All members of the host clan stood and swayed back and forth as they sang in harmony. "My little brother, where are you? Come back to me!" they sang over and over, varying the order of words a little and stressing various syllables.

As well as mourning, some songs related incidents from clan legends, often those concerned with the acquisition of a crest. Their words were not necessarily mournful, but the tunes and rhythms were somber. Most were accompanied by tambourine-type drums with deerskin heads. Some had crests painted inside the drumhead, where they would not be worn off from being beaten.

While the Grizzly Bears sang their clan songs, the host women danced. They wore cloth headbands with feathers inserted and long beaded earrings, and their faces were painted with designs of the clan crest. One woman had a stripe of red the width of her eye painted from the hairline down to the mouth and then across the lips and chin, depicting the upright bar of the killer whale's dorsal fin. Another had a narrower red stripe from hairline to chin passing over each eye, illustrating the vapor jet of the blowing killer whale.

Over their long skirts most of the women wore blankets of blue serge with red borders, and button designs of a killer whale or grizzly displayed on the backs. A few women of higher caste wore Chilkat blankets. When the floor was crowded, they danced only with their arms and body, not moving their feet.

Nobody left the potlatch while the songs were being sung. After the singing had gone on for many hours, the Frog clan chief Qoxkan addressed Kowishte.

"Would the Eagle chief step out of the way?" This was an acceptable way of asking for a recess.

The host chief Kowishte did not move, continuing instead to watch the activity. Recognizing this behavior as part of the protocol, Chief Qoxkan remained unruffled and did not repeat the request. A little later the host chief looked in the Frog chief's direction.

"I'll move out of your way," Kowishte said. Then everybody rose and went outside for half an hour.

On their return, the singing of memorial songs continued until all who wanted to commemorate their dead had sung. Kowishte then came forward to announce the names of honor he was bestowing on his grandchildren and nephews. But first Kitlen, the ranking member of the council of his brothers and sisters, came forward to address the Grizzly Bear host chief.

"You, my nephew, are now officially named head chief of the Grizzly Bear clan," Kitlen said. "After our honored chief's funeral ceremony, the council met to choose the nephew most worthy to succeed him. For your knowledge of clan traditions and devotion to clan customs, for your steadfast character and sense of what is right, and for your strength of body and will, you were chosen. Now that the anniversary potlatch has been given, you inherit the name acquired from the Blackfish people in battle and passed on through many Grizzly Bear chiefs."

At a signal from the song leader, the Grizzly Bear people broke out in song.

When the singing finished, Chief Kowishte spoke. "For this honor I thank all of you," he said. "I know what great responsibility this honor brings. To prepare for receiving it, I fasted many days before this potlatch. With the help of the Eagle, Grizzly, and Killer Whale spirits, I shall use all my strength and will to do what is best for the clan."

After the ceremony honoring him, the head chief called his nephews to him. The first to receive an honor name was Galge.

"On you, Galge, a most deserving nephew, I confer the name of Caxna, held by many ancestral Grizzly Bear chiefs." He then related some of the past leaders' achievements.

"Most honored Chief, I accept this revered name and the responsibility that goes with it," the subdued Galge replied. "I shall try to prove worthy of this honor."

One by one, Kowishte called other nephews to come forward to receive honor names. On two of Galge's companions he conferred the names of former chiefs Skillat and Shustaks. Then it was time to present the gifts.

RAVEN IN A FOG

While paddling along at sea Raven met his brother-in-law Petrel. "Where are you coming from in that fine canoe?" he asked.

"From over there," Petrel replied vaguely, wary of Raven, who had stolen water from his spring to create the rivers and streams.

Raven then began to question Petrel about events in the world, but with no greater success. Finally he asked, "Where were you born? How long have you been living?"

"Ever since the great One-Who-Lives came up from under the earth," Petrel answered.

"Why, that is only a few minutes," mocked Raven.

Petrel grew angry. "When were you born?" he asked.

"Before this world was known," said Raven.

"That is just a little while back," Petrel countered.

They continued in this way until both were enraged. Pushing Raven's canoe away from him, Petrel put on his fog hat, and immediately they were surrounded by fog. Raven could not see where he was and became frightened.

"My brother-in-law, you are older than I am," he shouted to Petrel. "You have lived longer than I."

Petrel took sea water and sprinkled it in the air so that it fell through the fog in a fine rain. Raven did not like that at all. Then after Petrel had had his fun, he took off the fog hat and could see Raven in his own canoe, peering in all directions. Raven called to him.

"Brother-in-law, you had better let that hat go into the world." So Petrel did, and created the mist and fog.

GIFTS AND PARTIES

Gifts at memorial potlatches were not made in payment of any particular service, but were given to acknowledge the guests' courtesy in attending, in listening to laments, in easing the hosts' grief by comforting speeches, songs, and dances. The gifts were also tokens of appreciation for the guests' witnessing of these events and validating the hosts' claims to the actual and symbolic possession of names, crests, songs, and other properties exhibited at the potlatch.

The final ritual of the memorial potlatch ceremony,

the distribution of gifts, was now at hand. Chief Kowishte studied the array of blankets, coppers, carved boxes and figures, tools and utensils, satisfied that each guest would receive a suitable gift and that nobody would be insulted by receiving one of too little value or burdened by the obligation of returning one of value beyond his means.

"I think it will go well," he murmured to Kitlen. "Then we can enjoy the next four days of feasting and entertainment by our guests."

As the people entered Hit Len to be seated in their ranking order, they glanced at the displayed gifts, indications of the donors' standing and generosity, and silently assessed the value of each as well as the means of its donor. A gift either above or beneath the means of the donor exposed him to ridicule. The quality of the gifts also suggested the value of the gift that viewers could expect and that they hoped would elevate their status.

When all were seated, Kowishte signaled the nakani to begin distributing the gifts. The nakani held each gift high for all to see and called out the donor's potlatch name. Then he named the deceased person for whom the gift was given and who received its spiritual benefit, just as he partook spiritually of the food eaten and tobacco smoked ceremonially. The living felt strongly the presence of their deceased relatives at the potlatch gathering. Finally the name of the guest receiving the gift was called, and he came up to accept it.

"With highest respect Chief Kowishte presents these five coppers." The nakani announced the first gift, pointing to five large copper shields held by young clan members nearby. "He presents them for his deceased uncle, former head chief of the Grizzly Bear clan, to our honored Frog clan guest, Chief Qoxkan of Copper Plate House."

The crowd remained silent as the Frog clan chief rose to accept his gift, proceeding to the other side of the house where the nakani stood by the door. All looked with admiration at the burnished copper shields, each three to four feet high, and with equal admiration at the chief.

The Frog people especially rejoiced, as these esteemed coppers were now the property of their clan and would greatly increase clan wealth and prestige. Kowishte, too, was pleased, knowing these prestigious gifts that added to the status and wealth of the Frog clan would make it an even more formidable ally of the Grizzly Bear clan.

When Qoxkan reached the place where the nakani stood, he bowed slightly toward the Grizzly Bear chief and then addressed him.

"Honored Chief Kowishte, the Frog people accept with highest respect your very generous gift, and with it we will revere the memory of your deceased uncle. This gift adds to the wealth and prestige of the Frog clan, and the honor you do us in giving it further strengthens the bond between our clans. We shall place these shields with our other treasured crest objects—the greatest of which is the Frog." Then he began to relate the story of how the clan took the frog as their crest.

■ ■ ■

A man and his wife were crossing the mouth of a bay, when the fog began to close in around them. Soon it became so thick they could not see, so they stopped paddling and sat, idle, in their canoe. Then faintly in the distance, they heard singing. The song gradually became loud enough for them to make out the words.

"We picked up a man. You picked up a man," the first verse repeated over and over. Soon they were able to make out the words of the second verse.

"They captured a man. They captured a man. You captured a man." These phrases were also repeated in a voice by this time so powerful it echoed among the mountains. The singing went on for such a long time the man and wife found themselves joining in.

As the fog began to rise, the voice seemed to come closer. Now able to scan the water, they finally found the source: a frog swimming along the shore. Amazed that this small creature seemed to produce such vast echoes of song, the couple turned in its direction and paddled alongside it for some time. Once sure of the source of the singing, the man scooped up the frog and staked his claim to it.

"This frog is going to be mine."

"No, it is going to be mine," his wife countered. "I am going to claim it." Their dispute lasted for some time until the man finally gave in to his wife.

When the couple reached the shore of their village, the wife lifted the frog as if it were her child and carried it to a lake, where she put it down gently and spoke to it.

"This will be your new home, here on this lake near the Frog clan village, and their people will hold you in high regard and will honor you as their crest."

■ ■ ■

Dog Salmon Chief Tanaxk of Til Hit was next called, and again there was a hush as the chief of Kowishte's wife's clan came forward.

"With greatest respect Chief Kowishte presents you, Chief Tanaxk, with four copper shields," the nakani said. All gazed with admiration at the Dog Salmon chief and his new possessions.

"Honored Chief," Tanaxk said, turning to address

Kowishte. "We of Til Hit thank you for your great generosity in bestowing these valuable gifts on our clan. We shall hold them in highest regard." Then he began to relate the story of his clan crest, the Dog Salmon.

∎∎∎

A small boy and his friends were snaring seagulls on a beach near a stream where their families had set up the summer fishing camp. Becoming hungry, the boy ran into the house to ask his mother for something to eat. His mother gave him a piece of dried salmon which had a little mold on one end.

"Why do you always give me the moldy end of the salmon?" the boy complained, throwing the fish into the corner. When he returned to the beach, he found that he had snared a seagull. Wading out to the snare, he tried to pull in his catch, but the bird proved stronger than he and pulled him out to sea, where he sank.

When the boy did not return for dinner, his parents became concerned. They looked for him on the beach, then scoured the woods and called at the neighboring houses. They then went down to the water's edge where the boy had been baiting his traps, and saw his tracks leading into the water. Following the shore, they searched for him for several days without eating or sleeping. Though they returned to camp and fished the rest of the summer, they kept on looking for their son. But when it was time to return to their winter home, they had to end the search.

The boy had been captured by the Salmon People, who had swum out to him when he sank. They took him to their village, but once there, his captors appeared to be human beings. The Salmon People named him Moldy End because of his complaint about the dried salmon his mother

81

had given him, and kept him for over a year.

Moldy End was not happy and was hungry all the time. But a Salmon person who had befriended him gave him a small stone to put in his mouth.

"Salmon never eat when they are on their way to the spawning grounds," his friend explained. "We just hold a stone in our mouths to keep us from getting hungry." Moldy End became more cheerful and wandered over to the edge of the village to watch the Herring People dancing next door. One of the women came over to talk to him.

"Do you remember when you said something insulting about the salmon?" she asked, careful not to repeat the exact words herself for fear of offending the Salmon People. "That is why they have captured you."

"You seem to be awfully hungry," she continued. "Go over to the creek there and catch a small salmon and roast it on a stick in the fire. But be sure to pick up all the skin and bones and return them to the creek."

Moldy End did as the woman said and satisfied his hunger for a while. But in picking up the salmon remains, he did not see a small bone from around the eye fall into a hole. That night the chief's son was ill with a sore eye.

"Let's go look around the fire and see whether you overlooked part of the fish remains," Moldy's Salmon friend suggested. When they found the bone and threw it into the creek, the chief's son got better and his eye no longer hurt.

When spring came, the salmon prepared to return to the streams to spawn and they took Moldy End with them. The chief took his people to the creek where Moldy End's parents had again set up their summer camp and were fishing. As the salmon entered the mouth of the creek where his parents had set their nets, Moldy's mother spotted a large, silvery dog salmon.

"Look at that beautiful salmon!" she said to her husband. "Catch it!" The husband speared the fish and brought it to his wife. When she started to bring her knife down on the fish's neck to cut off its head, she struck something hard.

"What's this?" she asked.

"It looks like a piece of copper," her husband said. Examining the fish closely, they saw a chain around its neck.

"It's our son's copper necklace!" she exclaimed, when she realized what she had.

Surmising that this salmon was their lost son, they prepared a cedar bark mat with down and laid the fish upon it, and then put the mat on the roof of the house. Inside the house the shaman sang his spirit songs to bring the boy's spirit back in his human form. Toward morning the people inside the house felt the roof shake and went out to see what had happened. The boy's father arrived in time to see the salmon's head turning into a human one. Then as the singing continued, other parts of the salmon's body gradually changed, until it had become entirely human.

"I am Moldy-End-of-Salmon," the boy said to those gathered around him. Then the other spirits that had come to dwell in him during his stay with the Salmon people spoke.

"I am Herring Spirit," one said.

"I am Crane Spirit," said another.

"I am Salmon-People's-Canoe Spirit," said a third.

When he had fully regained consciousness, Moldy End told his parents and friends of his experiences and of the things he learned from the Dog Salmon People. When he grew up he became a successful shaman. His family and their descendants took the Dog Salmon for their crest. To this day the Dog Salmon people are always careful to place all the remains of salmon they have eaten back into the creek so the salmon will revive and return to the creek again the following summer.

■ ■ ■

After Tanaxk had taken his seat again, Frog Chief Qalaktc of Gagan Hit was called and presented with one shield and several blankets.

"Highest Grizzly Bear Chief, the Frog people of Gagan Hit and other houses of the village thank you for your generous gifts," Qalaktc exclaimed. "These gifts do honor to you and to all of our clan."

"In the early days, when coming down from the North," Chief Qalatkc went on, "the Frog people first settled close to the Grizzly Bear village before the great avalanche buried most of the clan and caused the rest to move to our present village. I will tell you the story of these early Frog people, which now belongs to all the Frog clans."

■ ■ ■

A youth was walking through the woods when a frog crossed his path. Unhappy because he had had poor luck in hunting, the young man kicked the frog out of his path and went on his way, not noticing that the small creature had landed on its back and was kicking frantically to turn itself over. Had this young man been living according to clan customs, he would not have mistreated any creature that way, especially a frog. For as the crest animal of his clan, the frog is held in highest regard and treated with greatest respect. But the young man was too much absorbed in competing with his cousins to give much thought to what is right.

A few steps farther along the trail, the young man
tripped and landed on his back. He lay there awhile to

regain his breath and then tried to get up. But he could not move his arms or his legs or even raise his head. His senseless body just lay like a stone on the ground. When he tried to call out to his relatives in case they were nearby, he could neither open his mouth nor make any kind of sound.

Much later in the afternoon his cousins, following the same trail home, came upon his inert body. "Look at our cousin asleep on the path," called the first one to see him.

"He was in such a hurry to get back before us that he wore himself out," another scoffed, prodding the unconscious man with his foot. But the man could not hear their taunts, nor could he move in any way. So they lifted him up and carried him back to the village.

The unconscious young man was able, however, to hear the Frog People conversing, because his spirit was still in their realm. For when he had fallen, they had captured it and tied it to a house post.

"Let him starve right there where he is tied," one angry Frog person snarled.

"No, don't let him starve," advised a more cautious one. "Let's feed him and then see what the chief says."

So they fed their captive and went in search of the chief, but he had not yet returned from a canoe trip to canvass the islands for deer. They settled down to wait. Finally they heard somebody calling from the beach.

"Here comes the canoe of Chief Frightful Face!" the voice announced. The Frog men hurried down to greet the chief and help his companions carry the canoe above the tide line. Then they walked with him to his house, telling as they went about their capture of the man who had mistreated the frog.

"This man insulted us," one explained. "He threw one

85

of our women down and kicked her over onto her back. We have tied him to a post in my house."

"Untie the captive and bring him here," said the chief, and they went to do as he ordered.

When the chief saw the captive, he recognized him as a Frog person from another village and became angry.

"Why have you mistreated Woman-in-the-Road?" he asked. "She and all of us belong to the same clan as you."

The young man could only stand before the chief in stunned silence. He did not remember meeting a woman. He could only remember seeing a frog in his path and kicking it out of his way. Now he was sorry and ashamed he had lost his temper and been cruel to the small creature.

Then the chief ordered the young man to return to his own village. "Go! You have disgraced yourself as well as us."

The man started out of the Frog chief's house but suddenly found himself lying in his own house, in his own village, with his relatives standing around him. For as soon as he had been dismissed from the Frogs' house, his spirit returned to his body, which was lying where the villagers had placed it after carrying him home.

"Look! He's coming to!" one of the women called out. As he regained consciousness, he sat up and tried to move his hands, then his legs. They worked fine. Finally he spoke.

"How did I get back here?" he asked those gathered around watching his reactions.

"We carried you back," a cousin answered.

"From the Frogs' house?" he asked, amazed.

"No," they laughed. "From the trail where you fell."

The young man was still puzzled. Had he been dreaming or had he actually been to the Frogs' house? If so, how did he get back? The relatives were amused, thinking his confusion was due to having been unconscious. But this uncle was more serious.

"What's this about a frog?" he asked.

The young man then repeated what he remembered of his experience.

"Are you certain the frog called himself a Frog person?" the uncle interrupted, when he told of the Frog chief's scorn.

"I am certain," the young man replied.

"And then he let you return to the village because he said you belonged to the same clan as he?" Again the young man agreed.

"This is a very strange thing," the uncle mused. "Despite your insult, this Frog Chief befriended us and spared your life. Henceforth the frog shall be our crest animal and shall be held in highest regard by all of us. Let us go compose a song to commemorate this experience and pay homage to the frog."

■ ■ ■

Chief Qalaktc ended his story. "This is how our people became the first to adopt the frog for their crest animal," he explained to the gathered clans.

The nakani then called the other Frog house chiefs in order of status and presented them with gifts, one copper shield to the highest of them, blankets and carved boxes to the others. These items were considered clan property and would be taken home to put on display and be given as gifts by that clan in the future. Carved dishes, baskets, and jewelry were kept as personal gifts. Each chief thanked the nakani profusely for the gifts. Finally the rank and file were summoned.

When the gifts were all distributed, the guests were

invited to a feast the next day so all could forget their sor-
rows. This was the first of four days of feasting, the first and
last nights at Hit Len, the house of Kowishte, now acknowl-
edged as clan chief, the other nights in houses of other
Grizzly Bear chiefs. The guests performed entertaining
songs and dances for the hosts in appreciation of the feasts
and gifts. These feasts were also the occasion of competitive
dances, both group and solo, where the contestants outdid
one another in violent movements and shouting.

The nakani maintained order by formally leading each
group into the hall and watching over events from the doorway. If quarrels broke out, they asked for peace in the name
of the deceased ancestor whose ceremonial garments the
dancers were wearing. To keep the various dance groups
from making mistakes, which could provoke insults from
the opposing clan dancers and lead to fights and even wars
between clans, the nakani prompted the song leaders when
they needed it, especially if they were singing a host song. It
was a grave wrong for a song leader to forget something or
make an error, as it brought ridicule on the whole clan. To
prepare for perfect performances, song leaders fasted and
slept apart from their wives before the potlatch.

As a further measure to counter any hostility provoked
by rivalry, each group was expected to compose a peace song
for the children of the opposing clan. These songs express-
ing love and admiration for each other's children helped
reduce tension. "I am holding your daughter's hand," was an
often-repeated phrase of the children's songs.

The first to dance, the Frog clan group, backed onto
the stage in postures that immediately displayed the crest
symbols on their dance robes. At the head of the line the
group's leader wore an ermine headdress with ten long

ermine tails trailing down his back, and seal whiskers extending upward from his carved wooden raven frontlet.

But before they started to dance, Chief Qoxkan of Tina Hit stood before the group. His Chilkat blanket emblazoned with the Frog crest was draped over his shoulders, and he wore a wooden hat surmounted by the Frog. Qoxkan waited for silence and then began a second story of how his clan acquired the Frog crest.

■ ■ ■

In the woods behind the houses at the Grizzly Bear village lay a big lake filled with frogs. The frogs often sat on a raised marshy mound in the middle.

One day the chief's daughter Qaltsixkli was walking in the woods with her sister. She came upon a frog, picked it up, and examined it.

"There are so many of these creatures—I wonder if they reproduce like human beings?" she said to her sister. "I wonder if men and women cohabit with them?"

The woman's boldness frightened her younger sister. "You had better be careful," she replied. "You might be punished for your disrespect."

"Oh, it's just a frog," Qaltsixkli laughed, as she dropped the small creature to the ground. But her sister's remarks had dampened her spirits. "Let's go back," she said suddenly, and they returned home.

That night Qaltsixkli was walking down toward the beach in front of her house. She should not have been out alone, but this self-willed young woman hardly worried about what was proper, and she felt she would be safe in front of her own house. Suddenly a young man came to her and boldly asked, "May I marry you?"

Qaltsixkli was astounded, for she had never seen the

89

man before, and besides, young men did not approach young women in that way. Marriages were arranged by their aunts and uncles. Qaltsixkli, a chief's daughter, had had many offers of marriage. But none of the suitors had pleased her aunts, and Qaltsixkli was happy to be free. But now she was seized with a great longing to marry this stranger. Taking advantage of her hesitation, the young man pointed toward the lake.

"My father's house is right up here," he said, taking her hand and guiding her in the direction of the house. Curious, and enjoying the company of the handsome young man, Qaltsixkli went along with him.

"How fine it looks!" the girl replied as the house—or what appeared to be the house—came into view.

When they drew close, a door into the dwelling seemed to open for them. But in reality, the water at the edge of the lake had been raised like a curtain to let them walk under it. Once inside, the couple could see the Frog people, who looked like human beings to Qaltsixkli. She soon became so animated in talking with the many young people that all thoughts of her own home left her. The Frog people treated her like a princess, and she was happy to stay with them.

Meanwhile, her friends and family missed her, and for days hunted everywhere for her. "Qaltsixkli has been gone so long, something surely has happened to her," her father lamented.

"My daughter! My beautiful daughter!" her mother wailed. "I know she must be alive somewhere."

"How could she go so long without eating? Nor could she have survived the cold," the father said. Then he ordered the men to beat the drums for the mourning ceremony. The people cut their hair and blackened their faces with soot to mourn the loss of the chief's daughter.

The next spring a young man getting ready to go out hunting went up to the lake in the woods to make ritual preparations. He had to bathe in urine, which was believed to confuse animals and make them come in the hunter's direction. When the young man finished his bath and threw the urine into the lake, some of it fell on the frogs sitting at the edge of the water. Their sudden movement as they all dived at once amused the young man.

The hunter returned the next day and began to bathe again. Suddenly he noticed a woman among the frogs on the marshy mound in the middle of the lake. It looked like Qaltsixkli! The young man dressed, ran back to the village, and went right to the chief's house with his news.

The chief and his wife invited the young man in for dinner. When they had finished eating, he recounted his tale in further detail.

The chief and his wife were elated. That evening they left for the lake with their relatives. When they were close enough to make out the mound in the middle of the lake, they saw the woman among the frogs and recognized their daughter. Overjoyed, they called out and waved to her, but the daughter seemed not to hear or recognize them.

"Qaltsixkli!" her mother called. "Look at us. We're over here."

"We have come to take you home," her father added. But Qaltsixkli continued to sit like a princess on the mound, gazing serenely ahead, unaware of her parents' presence.

The chief and his relatives returned home with heavy hearts.

"Let us take the Frog people some gifts," his wife

suggested. "Maybe they will release our daughter to us."
The chief agreed.

The next morning the chief selected several carved
boxes, baskets, and blankets and set out with his relatives.
The Frog people accepted the gifts, leading the clan to
believe they would release the girl. But once they had the
gifts, they made no effort to return her.

Enraged, the chief and his family returned home.
During the night he worked out a plan to free his daughter.
The next morning he called all the men to him.

"The Frog people have refused to release my daughter
even though we gave them many valuable gifts," he told
them. "Now we will have to take her from them. We must
go up to the lake and dig drainage ditches out from it to
lower the water and allow us to get to my daughter and
rescue her." In no time the chief and his clan were at the
lake digging trenches.

When the Frog chief saw what was happening, he told
the people about it.

"The intruders are digging out our laid-up food," he
said, referring to the mud on the lake shore. "Soon the
water will drain from the lake and ruin our preserves." Then
he turned to his woman captive.

"Ask your people to take pity on us and spare our
lives," he implored her. The daughter did as the Frog chief
commanded.

"We will not kill any of you," the chief replied to her
request. "We want only our daughter."

In the meantime, the water flowed out of the lake,
taking Frog people with it in all directions.

"What will become of us?" the Frog people wailed, as
they were thrown up onto land. "We will all die without our

pond and without our food supply."

Even though our clan had spared their lives, the Frog chief made a last attempt to keep Qaltsixkli. He "dressed her up," that is, covered her completely with frogs, and perfumed her with their special odor. But when she was washed down the trench with her Frog husband, her relatives were able to pull her from the water.

At first the young woman had difficulty talking. She could answer their questions only with a croaking sound. Eventually she was able to speak, but she could not eat.

"Soon you will be better, dear," the mother comforted her and tempted her with her favorite foods. But to no avail. Then in desperation the mother ordered the servants to hang Qaltsixkli over a railing to drain out the food she had eaten at the Frogs' house. The people watched in horror as the mud began to drain out of her mouth and were relieved when it had finished. But poor Qaltsixkli was dead.

Her parents moaned with grief as the servants took the lifeless body of their daughter into the house. They had lost her for good this time.

■ ■ ■

"After the funeral, our clan agreed to take the frog as their crest, in memory of the chief's daughter. Because the woman had gone to live with the Frogs," Chief Qoxkan explained, "frogs can understand the speech of humans. And our clan can almost understand the frogs."

When the chief finished his story, Frog clan dancers formed a semicircle on the dance floor. The leader sang the first phrase of a song and with his staff signaled the singers to join in. Spectators watched, acutely aware of every movement, dreading a false move or forgotten cue, for either of these could bring shame to the leader—and worse, conflict, if an opponent were to make a remark or give a sly look. The song leader had fasted before the potlatch and taken medicines to make him remember and to make him perform well and also medicines to make him win and to entertain well. Some dancers had taken medicine to make them feel joyful. Each clan had its own secret recipes for these herbal compounds made from forest plants.

The dancers swayed from side to side, using their bodies more than their feet, while keeping their feet firmly planted on the floor and their knees bent. At a signal from the leader, the dancers advanced or changed direction with a sudden hop, and the dance became more and more animated. Suddenly the music stopped and the dance was over. The Frog clan dancers' performance had been flawless.

Now it was the Dog Salmon people's turn. They too entered the room backwards, displaying the Raven and Dog Salmon emblems on their robes. Their leader wore the Chilkat blanket with a halibut design and the Raven hat.

The dancers had painted faces and wore tunics with clan crest designs. One man's face depicted the starfish torn up by Raven on his journey through the world: an orange X under each eye, orange lips, and a black tentacle curling from each side of his mouth. To help ensure peace, the dancers blew eagle down from pipes, scattering it over the spectators. Dog Salmon leaders had also fasted two days and taken appropriate medicines so that the dances would go smoothly and there would be no opportunity for ridicule. Under the eyes of the watchful nakani, dancers and singers on both sides contended to see who knew the greatest number of songs or who could dance for the longest time.

Women and children also took part in their dances, and between dances the host and guest chiefs exchanged complimentary speeches. One woman wore the flicker design on her face: several green and red lines going from the bridge of her nose to her hairline and from her lower lip to her chin. Similar marks streaked in a slant from her lower eyelids to her cheeks.

After the four days of feasting and dancing, Kowishte addressed his guests.

"I would like to thank all of you, especially those from distant places, for coming to the anniversary potlatch memorializing my uncle, our former head chief, and comforting us in our sorrow. We have joined in singing our most revered clan songs and retelling our clan histories and thus have formed a closer bond. You have honored us with your dancing, and for this I also thank you. For those of you who must return to your villages, we have prepared food and other provisions for your journey. The nakani will see that these things are delivered to your canoes. From the depths of our hearts we thank you."

All then returned to their homes and guest quarters to sleep, and all would rise early, the guests to board the canoes for home and the hosts to see them off. As they departed, the new Grizzly Bear head chief felt satisfied that the memorial potlatch for his uncle had gone well.

Kowishte knew that his guests probably had suspected that he also possessed the magical herbs that helped a man become rich. And he felt they probably agreed that the new Grizzly Bear chief was a man to be taken very seriously.

RAVEN LOSES HIS BEAK

As Raven was traveling around the world, he met some people who used whale blubber for bait. "Show me how you bait your hooks with that," he asked them, and then watched carefully as they wrapped the fat around their hooks. Later when they went out to fish, he hid behind the point and waited for them to drop their lines into the water. Then he dived into the water and nibbled the bait from their lines. Several times the fishermen, feeling the lines move, brought up the hooks. But they had nothing, and the bait was gone. Finally one jerked quickly and caught something. As he played his "fish," the line went under the boat, and Raven kicked hard against it to get loose. Suddenly his bill pulled out, and the fisherman reeled it in.

"Look at the Gonakadet nose I caught," he exclaimed. The men took this good-luck symbol to their chief, who sprinkled it with down and hung it on the wall.

Raven meanwhile found some spruce gum on the beach and made himself a nose. Pulling his spruce-root hat down over his face, he went up to the houses, determined to reclaim his own beak. He was directed to the chief's house and shown in.

"May I see the Gonakadet nose one of your fishermen caught?" he asked. Proud to show off his treasure, the chief handed it to Raven.

"I need more light. Can you open the smokehole?" No sooner did they do so than Raven slipped his beak into place and flew out the opening, leaving the people gawking in amazement.

PRESTIGE POTLATCH

T he funeral and the anniversary potlatches provided ceremonial opportunities for disposing of the deceased, paying those who performed the services, and honoring the dead, usually a renowned chief, as well as formalizing the accession to power of his successor. Both potlatches also earned prestige for the host clans.

But prestige alone was the principal reason for the third major potlatch type. Its main purpose was to enhance the political and social status of the host and the honored guests. It differed from the other two types in that the host gave the feast for his own children, rather than for his sisters' or brothers' children, although these nephews and nieces might also be honored with new names at the occasion. The host's clan rather than the host's wife's clan did the preliminary work involved in giving the potlatch, though both host and guest clans volunteered to build the house and raise the carved prestige pole, if there was to be one. And instead of slaves being killed, as at the funeral potlatch, they were freed, out of respect for the honored children.

The prestige potlatch also differed from the other types because everyone in attendance, guests and hosts alike, received gifts that were free of obligation to reciprocate at a future potlatch. Such unfettered generosity attested to the wealth and position of the host in his clan, while it contributed to the child's social rank in his own clan, adding to the status he already enjoyed through the position of his mother and her relatives. Both the father's and the mother's families also gained prestige from showing crest objects while singing songs and telling stories of their origins, and they reinforced their aristocratic status by restating clan rights to property, names, and crests.

At these lavish potlatches, guests were also honored and much property was given away and sometimes even destroyed, to display the host's wealth. Such conspicuous consumption made the host's riches seem limitless, and thereby raised the esteem in which he and his family were held. This increase in social status in turn translated into greater political power.

An important feature of the prestige potlatch was piercing the honored children's ears and conferring on each of them a renowned ancestor's name. Each such ceremony was recorded by adding a ring to the crown of the honoree's hat. A candidate for succession to the position of chief must have a multiringed hat, evidence of how many honor-name and ear-piercing potlatches had been given in his honor. A high number of ear piercings increased a young woman's eligibility for marriage to a chief. The more such potlatches a child was honored with, the higher his or her social and political status. Eight piercings, one ear piercing at each potlatch, was the ideal, though it was attained by very few.

Kowishte, the head Grizzly Bear chief, thought it was time to give a prestige potlatch for his son Gac, who was living with his uncle, the head chief of the Dog Salmon clan. The boy was showing promise of making an outstanding chief. Gac took clan tradition seriously. As a child he had been fascinated by the stories his grandmother told, especially those about heroes who became great chiefs. He had listened intently to narrations of their historic feats at other potlatches given by his uncle and his father, for he had ambitions of being a chief himself, and in his daily life he began to take these great men as models. Like the well-known hero Blackskin, who developed prodigious strength in order to tear in two the sea lion who had killed his uncle, Gac sat longer each day in the waters of the bay to build endurance and exercised vigorously to gain strength. Like Natsilane, the great seal hunter and craftsman who created the killer whale, Gac practiced patience and perfected his hunting and fishing skills. And like the boy Moldy End, he treated the salmon of his Dog Salmon crest as well as all other creatures with kindness and respect.

By adolescence Gac had developed a quiet but persuasive manner and a strong sense of what was right, as his father Kowishte had done. Even at this young age he showed good judgment and was fair in dealing with his

99

friends and relatives. Kowishte therefore decided to award him a special, honorary name at a potlatch.

Although Gac would be the honored guest, Kowishte wanted also to give recognition to his eldest daughter Yedecih, who at the age of ten had already won his admiration with her pleasant manner and her adeptness at acquiring the skills needed by a woman. She had learned to listen while others spoke and then to speak softly, always with tact and consideration. She had also learned not to be forward, especially where food was concerned, to wait to be invited to eat, and if she had food, to be willing to share it.

"Remember when the Boy-Who-Fed-Eagles was seeking a bride," her aunt had often told her. "He did not choose one of the two prettiest daughters as their father, the chief, had expected, but the one who showed restraint in eating and speaking." Though Yedecih knew well this story from her father's clan, she listened attentively while her aunt repeated it.

■ ■ ■

The Boy-Who-Fed-Eagles preferred to spear salmon and take them to the eagles out on the reef instead of helping to get food for the winter. When winter came, his family refused him food. Only an old aunt would slip him something to eat. When the family left for the eulachon fishing grounds, they left the boy and the old woman who had fed him behind without food or fire. But every day the eagles brought him salmon, halibut, seals, sea lions, whales, and other seafoods. Soon the old woman was able to cook on a fire started from an ember she had concealed in a clam shell. The rest she preserved and stored.

When the family returned, almost starved, since the eulachon run was poor, they were amazed at the young man's wealth. When the hungry people noticed grease on the water from fish and animals the young man had killed, they began to scoop it up and eat it greedily. The two prettier daughters, dressed in their finery, joined in this display of poor manners, but the oldest, plainer sister sat quietly in the canoe and did not eat until the young man had invited the family into the house for dinner. The young man chose her for his wife and also elevated his faithful old aunt to an esteemed position in his household.

■ ■ ■

"If you learn clan stories and follow clan tradition, you will develop qualities to make you a good wife," the aunt concluded. This aunt would pierce her brother's children's ears at the potlatch. As Kowishte's eldest sister, she held the highest ceremonial role for a woman. She was the one who cut the umbilical cord of her brother's children when they were born, attended his girls during seclusion at puberty, and played an important role in their coming-out potlatch. She taught the girls things they would need to know as wives of high-ranking men.

Some of the skills Yedecih would need as a wife she had learned from helping her grandmother. She was already skillful at filleting and cooking or drying fish. She helped her grandmother gather and prepare spruce roots and was learning to weave mats and baskets from them. She and her grandmother picked berries or dug clams and then preserved them. Yedecih had already had her ears pierced three times and was eagerly awaiting the coming potlatch.

All the local clans would be invited, as well as the Dog Salmon clan from their own village farther north. The local Frog clan would be guests of honor and dance against the local Dog Salmon people.

At this potlatch, all other clans were guests, including other Grizzly Bear houses. Chief Kowishte called upon eight of the highest Grizzly Bear chiefs to act as hosts and to invite the guests. Like the nakani in other potlatches, these chosen messengers went to stand before each of the Dog Salmon and Frog peoples' houses, crying, "You are invited!" And each time the chief of the house accepted according to clan tradition. Then the host chiefs left for the village of the Box House Dog Salmon people to invite them and then escort them to the potlatch. The chiefs also prepared the gift and seating lists, giving careful attention to the status and wealth of each guest.

The morning after the Dog Salmon arrived from the north, formal ceremonies of arrival and welcome took place at the beach, the same as for the memorial potlatch. The Frog and Dog Salmon chiefs and their retinue, all dressed in ceremonial garments, cast off in their canoes to await the formal welcome by Chief Kowishte. The dancers, with faces painted, wore their costumes as they went up the beach for the peace songs and dances, performed first by the guests and then by the hosts. After the hosts sang the welcoming song and sprinkled the guests with eagle down, the dancers returned to their canoes. Chief Kowishte waded out to the canoe of the Dog Salmon head chief.

"To the warmest place under my wings, I welcome you," he intoned the ritual welcome, placing his hand on the side of the canoe. "To the warmest place under my feathers, I welcome you." After Chief Kowishte had repeated this song and gesture at each canoe, the guests brought the boats up to the beach, changed into ordinary clothes, and accompanied their hosts to his house.

At the door the host chiefs greeted the guests and

seated each chief and his group according to status. Only the hosts wore their ceremonial garments the first four days, which were given over to the serious songs and stories.

When these solemn ceremonies and tales were finished, Chief Kowishte's sons and daughters were brought in for the ear-piercing ritual. They approached in order of age, teenagers first, on down to toddlers. Gac led the group with Yedecih next and the others following. Gac, the ranking child with four ear piercings, had received honorary names from several illustrious ancestors at earlier prestige potlatches. But Chief Kowishte had selected a special name for his son at this one.

"You have been honored with a very fine name," he told Gac. "Katgatex was one of the first head chiefs of the Dog Salmon clan, and his name has been held by many great chiefs since his time. Now you must work harder than ever to develop strength of mind and body to be worthy of this name."

If Gac continued to build his strength through daily exercise and bathing and then distinguished himself in hunting and fishing, the renowned name of Katgatex would increase his chances of succeeding his uncle as head chief someday. He rose to address the assembly.

"The name of Katgatex brings me great honor but also great responsibility. I hope I can do justice to the trust you have placed in me and bring honor to the Dog Salmon clan." Then he told the story of the Salmon chief.

■■■

There was a fisherman who fished only for salmon and nothing else. While walking along the beach one day after many days of stormy weather, during which he had caught nothing, he came upon a salmon left by the tide. As he **103** drew closer to it he was happy to see that it was fresh and undamaged.

"What a nice meal I shall have," he said to himself, bending down to pick it up. But he stopped suddenly as he heard the salmon speak.

"No, no! Don't eat me. I am chief of all the salmon. Put me back into the water. If you let me go, you will catch lots of salmon in the future." Though the man was sorry to give up the good dinner he had anticipated, the words of the salmon were persuasive, and he put it back into the water.

A short time later the weather that had made fishing impossible cleared, and the water became calm. The fisherman quickly collected his gear and headed out in his boat. Before long, he had a boatload of salmon. The next day, however, the bad weather had returned, and he was again unable to fish. As he walked along the beach and came to the place where he had found the salmon, he was surprised to see another large salmon lying in the same spot.

"What a fine-looking salmon," he said, "but I guess I have to put it in the water." As he carried it over to the water, he heard the salmon cry out.

"Oh no! Don't let me go," it pleaded. "Take me home and have me for supper. But after you have cooked me, don't break my bones. Handle them very carefully. Take the bones from my head and put them in a dish. Then put the dish under your pillow and sleep on them tonight."

The man brought the fish into the house and gave it to his wife to prepare, repeating the salmon's instructions. The woman handled the salmon very carefully. After cooking it, she removed the meat of the fish from its skeleton without breaking any of the bones. Then she set the head bones in a

dish, which she then put under their pillow, and that night

the husband and wife slept on the bones. When they awoke in the morning, they were amazed to see two tiny baby boys where the bones had been. The couple, who were childless but had been hoping for children for some time, were delighted to have two babies thrust into their care.

The boys grew rapidly and quickly acquired exceptional hunting and fishing skills. One boy was quiet and content to stay close to home. But his more adventuresome brother was restless, curious about what lay beyond their village. After begging his parents on many occasions to let him go off on his own, he finally won their consent.

The fisherman and his wife went about their everyday concerns and did not see the young man for several years. But word got back to them that their son had performed heroic feats in another village. He had saved the chief's daughter from death as she was being taken to a seven-headed monster that had plagued the village and demanded women victims to devour. Some time afterward this son sent word to his parents that the chief had given him this daughter in marriage.

At the death of the chief, who like the fisherman's son belonged to the Dog Salmon clan, this young man who married his daughter was named to succeed him. The new chief's father knew that the chief of all the Salmon had been reborn in his son.

■ ■ ■

As Gac finished his story, his father, Chief Kowishte, rose to address the group.

"In honor of my son Gac I have ordered three slaves released," he announced, to the approval of the assembly.

Yedecih was next to have her ear pierced. As she came forward, the honored aunt took hold of her earlobe, pierced it with a thorn, and drew a thread through the hole. During this process the crowd made a loud hissing sound, hoping to ease the pain. Then Kowishte stood before his daughter.

"Today I bestow on you the name of Yediwudugac, an ancestor renowned for her wisdom and balanced judgment," he said. "May her spirit enter into you." The assembly expressed surprise and pleasure at the announcement of this well-known and highly regarded name.

The ear-piercing ritual was repeated for each child and each was given an ancestral name, but none so esteemed as Yediwudugac.

The ear-piercing ceremony was followed by several days of songs, dances, and sumptuous feasting. The people ate dried salmon, halibut, seal, and bear meat dipped in eulachon oil. Herring roe and smoked fish and meat were also served. Berries of all kinds and a "whipped cream" made of soap berries added a sweet taste to the fare.

Following the feast, light songs and dances were performed, including special songs for children.

■ ■ ■

Tukaisînaʼt yēʼlî ctanūʼgya qōt uwatīʼ îdaʼyu tutaʼnk ʟ!enēdî yaʼtq!î.

You make me feel as if I were shaking, thinking about you, Dog Salmon children.

Lîdāʼl ye q!ayaikāʼq ʟ!enēʼdî yaʼtq!î. Līngît-aʼnî tu qoaʼnî yayiʟāʼk.

Do not talk anymore, Dog Salmon children. You are ahead of all the people in the world.

■ ■ ■

After the singing and dancing had gone on for some time, the host chiefs distributed gifts. Copper shields, many blankets, and large woven baskets were lavished on the chiefs of each clan as well as on the host's Grizzly Bear clan. Then the guests all left for home. Those who had a long way to go left with food and provisions, as was the custom, to sustain them for the journey.

RAVEN AND THE MAGIC SEAL CATCHER

One day Raven was walking along the beach and saw a seal out on the rocks.

"I would like to have that seal for my supper," he thought. But as he went toward it, the seal disappeared into the water. A little farther along, he saw another seal but had no better luck getting close to it.

As he drew nearer the village, Raven saw a man carrying a club out to the water's edge. The man bent over and scooted the club out on the water, saying, "My little club, do you see that seal out there? Go get it!" The club floated out to the large seal and came back with it. "My little club, you have done well," the man said and set off for home with his catch.

"A magic seal catcher!" Raven thought. "With a club like that I could catch all kinds of seals." He followed the man, trying to come up with a plan to get the club from him, and was surprised to see him hang it on a tree. Pouncing on the club with glee, Raven ran down to the water to send it out toward a seal.

"My little club, do you see that seal out there? Go get it!" he commanded, careful to use the man's exact words. But the club floated aimlessly. He tried again in his most persuasive manner, but to no avail. Then he became angry. "Get out there stupid club and do your job!" he shouted, but the club kept bobbing in the water.

In a fit of fury, Raven grabbed the club he had so coveted and began beating it against a rock, until finally it lay in pieces at his feet.

PEACE CEREMONY

After a war between two clans, the peace or "deer" ceremony, a thoughtfully designed ritual with elaborate symbolism, was employed to formalize the conditions of peace and erase all hostilities. Related to the potlatch, it also lasted eight days, included singing and dancing, and ended with a feast. Although the people often casually referred to it as a potlatch, in the peace ceremony there were no formal welcoming rituals, no dances on the beach at the arrival of the guests, and no preliminary parties in their honor. It was, rather, a solemn affair, during which only the "hostages" were allowed to sing and dance. No ancestral stories were told and no gifts were given after the feast.

The symbolic hostages were high-ranking members of the clan that was invited to the peace ceremony. If both clans taking part in the ceremony were from the same town, hostages were taken by members of the two clans in the course of a mock battle staged in the center of town. Otherwise those hostages were agreed upon by each clan, and the "guest" hostages went to the village of the clan hosting the ceremony, generally the aggrieved party, the one that felt it had suffered the greater loss in whatever altercation had taken place. Once the nakani had negotiated a settlement, they were responsible for making arrangements for taking hostages, also called "deer" because of that animal's gentle and guileless nature. Hostages were picked for their wisdom and stability as well as for their high rank and status, two each from the two clans seeking peace.

Before the peace ceremony began, all terms of the settlement had to be agreed upon by the two warring clans. To eliminate all causes for future conflict, the original reasons for the fighting had to be examined and restitution made for everything lost or destroyed, including human life. Nakani conducted these negotiations, the high-ranking men married to women of the clan they would represent and who therefore had a stake in seeing that the differences were resolved equitably. The nakani themselves could not belong to either side involved in the conflict but functioned as attorneys, negotiating according to Tlingit code. They met with both sides, learned the demands of the side with the greatest losses, and arranged for suitable compensation. Prisoners, scalps, and crests would be exchanged, but only after the killings had been equalized according to the number and rank of those killed. Thus the winner of the war generally became the loser of the peace, for the clan that counted more dead could demand from the other clan the lives of an equal number of men of the same rank and class. Sometimes two men of lower rank were accepted as compensation for one of high rank, although the aggrieved parties could sometimes be persuaded to accept a payment of property.

Wars or at least feuds between clans were fairly common, since any insult inflicted by a clan member, intentional or not, became a matter of clan concern. Insults included striking a person, calling him names, stealing his wife or his belongings, or damaging his property. Cutting a person's face was an extremely grave insult, as of course was murder. Warfare was also brought on by clan action, such as taking over another clan's hunting or fishing areas. Combatants battled with spears and knives before contact with outsiders made guns available. The heads of those killed in war were placed on posts in front of the victors' houses. Later the scalps, including all the hair and the ears, were cut off and treated with hot stones to remove the flesh. The scalps were then preserved with the clan's ceremonial garments and were worn by ranking clansmen on certain occasions.

Usually high-ranking members of the clan tried to achieve a peaceful settlement by offering payment of blankets or, in serious cases, coppers or slaves. On rare occasions crests, and with them stories and property, were given as ransom or in settlement of grievances. The peace ceremony was held to celebrate and sanction the final agreement.

It was to such a ceremony that the Grizzly Bear clan

had been invited by the Wolf clan to put an end to their bitter feud of many years' duration, starting early in Chief Kowishte's rule of over forty years and culminating in an attempt to make peace near its end. Numerous incidents of violence had led to retaliation on both sides, resulting in hundreds of deaths and rancorous hostility between the two groups.

The difficulty had begun when Wank, a Grizzly Bear man living in his Uncle Kagusak's house, became enamored of his uncle's wife and ran away with her. Upon learning the couple's whereabouts, Kagusak went to their village and sent word that he would like to talk with his nephew. When Wank came forward, his uncle lunged at him with a knife and slashed his face. As his nephew ran from him, Kagusak compounded the insult with a taunt, shouting after him, "Why are you running away?"

Unable to return home because of the stigma of these insults, Wank fled to the village of the Frog people, where he became friendly with some of the Wolf people living there. But before long he got involved with the Frog clan wife of a Wolf man and fled with her to a nearby bay. When the wronged husband found the couple, he demanded that Wank return his wife and pay proper restitution for the insult and the hardship he had caused. Instead of complying with the husband's wish, Wank shot and killed him and fled with the woman to another more distant bay, where his brother joined him.

Set upon revenge, the husband's Wolf clan relatives learned where the couple was staying and devised a plan to catch Wank. Some would lie in wait below the upper falls through which Wank had to take his boat to go hunting or fishing in outside waters; others would hide along the route

Wank would take if he escaped from the ambush at the falls. Knowing that the Wolf people would be looking for him and realizing they would try to trap him, Wank practiced swimming and diving daily to be able to escape readily. Each day he stayed longer under water until he could hold his breath for a very long time.

One day while Wank and his brother let their canoe down over the falls with a line, a Wolf man in hiding shot at them, killing the brother and wounding Wank in the leg. Wank dived into the rapids, swam a great distance under water before coming up, then continued to swim on the surface. But downstream another Wolf saw Wank, raised his rifle, and shot him. His lifeless body soon sank from sight.

On their way home, the Wolf men were asked by people they met, "Did you get any game?"

"Yes," they replied. "We shot a seal, and it sank." The people understood by this remark that Wank had been killed.

Upon learning of the killing of their two clansmen and the insult of their being called seals, the enraged Grizzly Bear people set out for the Wolf clan village to take revenge. They beached their canoe in an out-of-the-way place near the site, pulled it into the brush, and hiked through the woods to the village to avoid being recognized. Before long they met a Wolf man heading down the beach toward his boat. With one rifle shot they killed him, hurried back to their canoe, and pushed off for home. On the way they met people going toward the Wolf clan village.

"Have you met anyone on your trip?" the travelers asked, probably inquiring about relatives.

"Yes," the Grizzly Bear men answered. "We saw a halibut." When the remark was repeated to the clan leaders, they knew one of their men had been killed.

A few years later, it was rumored that the Wolf clan was seeking peace. Galge mentioned this matter to Chief Kowishte, who was getting ready for a trading trip by river and then overland to the head of the Nass.

"Do you take seriously this rumor of a peace mission by the Wolf clan?" Galge asked his uncle.

"I have not received any word that nakani are coming to negotiate demands with us, and there is little chance that peace overtures will be made during my absence," Kowishte told his nephew. So the chief and his company set out on their journey. Galge, by now a house chief himself, remained behind as ranking Grizzly Bear chief, since Kitlen, Kowishte's uncle, had died the previous year.

While Kowishte was away, the Wolf people, possibly on a peace mission, came to an island at the mouth of the river and set up camp. Then they took their canoes over to a more distant island where the Grizzly Bear people were catching eulachon and drying salmon. The eulachon, rendered for its oil, was cooked in water heated with hot rocks from the fire. The oil was skimmed from the water and stored in boxes to harden. The resulting delicacy was a staple in all Tlingit households and a valuable item of trade with people of the Interior.

When the Wolf people landed on the island near the Grizzly Bear fishing camp, most of the Grizzly Bear men were off in the canoes to find rocks to heat for rendering the eulachon. If the Wolf men had originally come for peace, this opportunity for revenge banished any such intentions, and the visitors quickly captured the women and the few men there. One man, however, managed to escape and alert the Grizzly Bear men on their return.

The Wolf people went back to the first island with their hostages, among them the noted old warrior Chief Yantancit, who had stayed in camp. Answering their taunts and insults with fiery responses, Yantancit let his captors know that his people would come to rescue them. His captors merely laughed and continued to ridicule the old man.

"They will have a long wait until the tide is high enough to land here," they jeered. The low tide had left long sandy flats around the island as far as they could see. But being strangers to the place, they did not know that a tidal slough running behind the island allowed canoes to beach even at low tide.

The returning Grizzly Bear people, warned by the man who had escaped, paddled their canoes stealthily to the beach on the back side of the island. As they came ashore, a sister of Yantancit thrust a gun into her son's hands. "Get this gun to your uncle," she ordered. "If you fail, I'll cut your head off!"—a threat meant to embolden the boy.

The Grizzly Bear people soon crept close enough to the Wolf people's camp to make out Yantancit among the captors. The boy suddenly dashed as close as he could, shouting, "Yantancit! You'll make a fine slave for the Wolf clan!"

Infuriated at the insult, Yantancit broke from his astonished captors and rushed at his nephew, who then thrust the gun into his uncle's hands. It was usually Yantancit's place to fire the first shot in battle, and that honor went to him now. With the five bullets in his gun, he killed five men. The Grizzly Bears took cover and none were wounded in the Wolf clan's return volley. When the Wolf people's guns were empty, the Grizzly Bears then fired, killing still more.

115

The incoming tide forced the fighting farther inland to a knoll that penned the enemy and made them easy targets as they tried to scale it. Finally a woman called out that all had been killed. When the Grizzly Bear men went over the rise to view the situation, they found that all were slain but some chiefs who had escaped to caves by using the dead as shields. They now came out to surrender.

The Grizzly Bear people held their captives in the fishing village on the island, waiting for Kowishte's return from the Nass before deciding what to do with them. But when a month had passed without word from him, Galge met with other house chiefs to determine the captives' fate. Lacking Kowishte's iron-handed leadership or the advice of the wily Kitlen, the council decided to send the captives home. The Wolf men were given a canoe, a gun, food, and provisions and told to make their way home.

On Chief Kowishte's return, Galge reported to him. "About one hundred Wolf men died without any losses on our side, but to avoid further anger from the Wolf clan, we sent the rest home."

"You should have killed them all," the outraged chief thundered. "For some day the Wolf clan will return to get even. Well, let them come! I have been laying in guns and powder and supplies for months. We are prepared for war."

But many years went by without incident. The younger Grizzly Bear people, not even born at the time of the original trouble, were inclined to believe that their relations with the Wolf clan had returned to normal.

But the Wolf people were biding their time. In the Wolf village there lived a young man, Yakwan, who had since birth been told the story of the slaughter of his clansmen by the Grizzly Bear people. Displaying traits of a good warrior at an early age, he was trained from youth to excel physically and mentally. He became especially proficient with the spear, handling the heavy weapon with ease and grace and throwing it with terrible power. His strength and fighting ability far outshone the skills of any other man. His Wolf clan aunts and uncles saw in Yakwan their hope for vengeance against the hated Grizzly Bear people.

The Wolf people laid their strategy with great care. When they felt that Yakwan was ready to lead them in battle, a group went in canoes to trade with the Grizzly Bears. They were received graciously and brought out the mountain goat wool they had got from the Chilkat to trade for eulachon oil. The day proceeded peacefully, and the two groups parted on friendly terms, with the Wolf people inviting their hosts to pay a return visit. When some Grizzly Bear people went several weeks later to trade with the Wolf clan, they too were treated with friendliness and respect. And since the trading went mostly in their favor, they returned home with good reports.

The following spring the head chief of the Wolf clan, Lex of Tcakkudi Hit (Eagle's Nest House), sent word that his clan would like to formalize a peace treaty. Many of the Grizzly Bear people were delighted, but Chief Kowishte was skeptical.

"The Wolf people have lost almost one hundred more men than we have. They are going to demand the sacrifice of many high-ranking Grizzly Bear people to even the numbers of dead," he warned. Kowishte was older than most of the council, but he had lost none of the astuteness that had made him such a powerful leader for so long. Most of the council members, however, wanted to believe that the Wolf people were sincere.

117

"They ask that we send deer for a peace dance," one of the chiefs said.

"The Wolf clan took the first step in restoring friendly relations when they came here to trade," another chief added. "And they invited us to their village."

"But no formal negotiations for restitution have been made between our nakani and theirs," Kowishte replied.

"They were very respectful to us when we traded in their village, and they allowed us much profit," a younger chief countered. The younger members were eager to resume peaceful relations with the Wolf people at the least cost to their own clan. Even the older Grizzly Bear chiefs who had reservations had to agree there seemed to be no honorable way to refuse the Wolf clan's invitation.

"I hope their present intentions are as noble as their recent actions," Kowishte commented. "Those chosen as deer should go realizing they might not return alive."

The mood was somber during the selection of hostages. Their wives were to accompany them. "It would be better to be killed with my husband," said one, "than to remain here as a widow." Many other relatives also decided to accompany the hostages and witness the ceremony.

As the canoe departed for the Wolf clan village, its passengers sang mourning songs.

■ ■ ■

Tcuc ya´odawūʟ ʌsî´ niyʌti´ tc!ʌ ʌtsū´x ī´wana, Nanyaā´yi yʌ´tq!î. Tc!a qā gōdjî´ gâ´s!ʌs gadustī´ntc.

You are hurrying to your death too fast, Grizzly Bear children. You ought to have thought longer about it.

■ ■ ■

Another addressed the enemy:

Yē´gî yêx ʌckādê´ yanaʌ´t Kā´gwʌntān yʌ´tq!î dātuwu´.

*Hātsatîya´ Kā´gwAntān yA´tq!î gūsu´ xān îkgwAnā´wu
kayaqayî xadē´s ādushā´îtc?*

Thinking of you Wolf Clan children is like having spirits come down on me.

Why don't you keep your promise of dying with me?

■■■

Upon arrival the Grizzly Bear people were met by their hosts and taken to the Wolf chief's house. All the proprieties of the peace ceremony were observed. The hostages were dressed in fine clothes, seated on luxurious blankets in places of honor, and given honorific names. A special song was composed for each to sing.

A taboo forbade the hostages from doing anything for themselves. Servants fed them and even combed their hair. Feathers in the form of a V were placed in a headband on their foreheads, and down was sprinkled on their hair to encourage peace-keeping behavior. Like adolescent girls in seclusion, they were allowed to talk only to their attendants and to eat only certain foods. They were not allowed to look at their wives during this period. They had to emulate the gentleness of deer in their speech and actions, to be the epitome of peacefulness. Their attendants watched them carefully for any sign of hostile speech or behavior. The hostages were each given a round stone to rub on their mouths every morning before the raven called, to ensure that they would not say anything offensive during the day.

The peace ceremony was to last four days rather than the usual eight because the hostages had traveled from another village. On the first day of captivity, the deer fasted. Ceremonial dancing began on the second night. Hostages from both clans took turns doing their songs and dances, supervised by the nakani. The hostages stood facing the wall, their backs to the spectators, each flanked by attendants. Next, each deer sang the song specially written for him. Then, before facing the people of the captor clan, he did a traditional turn counterclockwise, or "sunwise," in a circle as a peace symbol. Other clan songs were sung, usually the same ancient songs sung for mourning. After three days of singing and dancing by the deer, a feast would be held.

Each day of dancing went by in the manner of all peace ceremonies. When the hostages of the Grizzly Bear danced, their hosts sat in serene appreciation. "How needless our fears were," they said to one another. "It will be good to have peace with the Wolf people again."

The feast after the last dance would mark the end of the ceremony. Now the deer were doing their final dance. Concentrating intently on each movement, they did not see Yakwan come and stand in the doorway. Suddenly he raised his spear over his head, and the Grizzly Bear witnesses to the ceremony gasped. Weapons were not permitted at a peace ceremony.

But this was not to be an ordinary peace ceremony. This was the moment Yakwan had been trained for since childhood, for which he had sat long hours in icy water, run long distances, and practiced daily with his spear until he excelled above all others. Now he took aim at the unsuspecting deer. In a matter of minutes the rest of the Wolf men joined in to massacre all the Grizzly Bear people who had come, including the women. Only two men who had not attended the final peace dance escaped death; they hurried home in their canoes to relay the story of the massacre to their clansmen.

The Wolf people took the dead over to an island and unloaded their bodies onto the beach. No funeral pyres were lit. There was no burial ceremony or feast or songs. The bodies of their enemies were exposed for the birds and animals to devour, leaving their spirits to wander the earth until proper burial rites were held. The Wolf clan returned to the chief tribal house to celebrate their victory with a feast. When everyone had eaten, Yakwan's uncle, their head chief, rose.

"Today my nephew Yakwan has avenged the Grizzly Bear clan's slaughter of our Wolf brothers so many years ago. Though those killed today do not number so many as our men lost, the hearts of the Wolf people can rest easier knowing that the blood of high-ranking Grizzly Bear people has been shed to compensate for the deaths of Wolf clan people. Again we can hold our heads high under the revered crest of the Wolf. Grizzly Bear people will no doubt come to seek revenge. But now we have the great warrior Yakwan to fight against them."

The chief then began the story of how the Wolf came to be their crest.

■ ■ ■

While camping out on a hunting trip, a man was loading his boat with his catch when he saw a wolf coming toward him. As the wolf drew closer, the man noticed that it showed its teeth as if it were laughing. The wolf approached him in a shy manner, so the man was not wary of it. Instead he looked closely at the wolf's mouth and saw that it had a bone stuck between its teeth, which kept its mouth from closing. The man took the wolf's head in his hands and then gently pulled on the bone, twisting it a little to make it come out.

"Now you must show me what makes you such a lucky hunter," he said, but the wolf just turned and walked away

121

from him. The next night the man dreamed that he had come to a very fine town, one that he had never seen. It was only when the wolf that he had befriended came to greet him that the man realized he was in the Wolves' town.

"Now I shall tell you something that will make you very lucky," the wolf said to the man. "From this time forward, I am your friend. I am grateful for what you did for me and I shall be your friend always."

Shortly afterward the man returned to his village and, after unloading his catch, went to the chief's house to tell him about his unusual experience. The chief listened intently to the man's story and then thought for a while.

"This is a good sign. We must adopt the wolf for a clan crest. We will treat the wolf with respect and it will be our guardian."

■ ■ ■

When the head chief had finished his story, another chief came forward to tell the story of the Brown Bear.

"Although the wolf is our main clan crest," he explained, "the Wolf people also claim the Brown Bear as a second crest. Our claim is based on the experience of early clan members with Kats and his children." Then he began the tale.

■ ■ ■

Kats was a man of our clan who went on a hunting trip with his dogs. While the dogs were chasing a male bear, the bear's wife lured the man into her den and hid him from her husband. Kats was surprised to see the female bear take off her skin coat once they were inside the cave. She looked just like a woman. He remained with the bear woman for several years and they had many children.

From time to time, however, Kats grew lonely and

went to visit his own people. The bear wife allowed him to do so, but warned him not to touch his human wife or pick up his human children. On his way back to the bears' home from one of these trips, Kats would usually go out for seal, sea lions, and other animals, which he carried by canoe to the inlet where his bear wife waited for him. Their children would go down to the beach and, with the rough actions of young bear cubs, pull the canoe ashore and unload the game, throwing it from one to another and up to their mother. Because of the cubs' rough actions, the Wolf people had a saying: "If you think you are brave, be a steersman for Kats."

But one day, on returning to his original village, Kats saw one of his human children and, overcome with emotion, swept the child into his arms and held it to him. Later, on his way back to his bear family, Kats made the usual stops to hunt and took the game to the inlet where his bear wife lived. When he saw the cubs running toward the canoe, he started to unload the game for them to take to the cave. Instead the cubs grabbed the hunter and tossed him from one to another and up to their mother the way they usually threw the game. But Kats died from their rough handling.

As the bear children matured, they scattered all over the world and came to their deaths in various places. These children were among the bears our clansmen sought out and slew for having killed some of our fishermen. Once when the Wolf people were getting herring at Town-at-the-Mouth-of-the-Lake, their herring disappeared while it was being dried before the fire. They did not realize that a bear had wandered into their camp, reached down through the smokehole, and taken it.

"Who is this thief that is stealing all the fish?" the

fishermen asked. The bear resented being called a thief and killed the fishermen in anger.

When the Wolf people in the village realized what had happened, they vowed revenge. They took their spears and set out to kill all the bears in the area where the people had been gathering herring. They discovered the bears hiding in holes they had dug.

"Come out and defend yourselves," the Wolf clan leader called to the bears. It did not take long for the people to kill all of them. But when they realized that these bears were the children of Kats, they took their skins and heads off and preserved them. These were treated with honor and respect, and the Brown Bear became a Wolf clan crest.

■ ■ ■

By the time the chief had finished his storytelling, it had become quite late. "This has been a good day for the Wolf people," he told the gathered clan. "Let us go to our homes now knowing we have regained our honor."

But time would show that honor had not been served. Serious breaches of ritual had occurred, and the consequences would reverberate for decades in the form of ill-will and violence between the two clans. Only if the peace ceremony had been approached by both sides with unanimous good intentions, and without the compromise of required procedures, could it have succeeded. But as it was, no wrongs had been redressed nor equitable settlements made. For the peace ceremony was not a treaty or a means of settling conflicts. It was, rather, the confirmation of a series of prior agreements negotiated by the nakani. To restore peace between two warring clans, nakani from both sides had to hear grievances and bring the two parties to agree on restitution; they had to make sure the irritant was removed so the wounds of conflict could heal. The first step in this healing, the peace ceremony was a celebration of a treaty between two warring parties. When properly carried out, the peace ceremony, like the traditions and observances of the potlatch, became a vehicle for maintaining order and good will among individuals and clans in the volatile Tlingit society.

FURTHER READING

Andrews, C. L. *The Story of Sitka*. Seattle: Lowman & Hanford, 1922.

_____. *Wrangell and the Gold of Cassiar*. Seattle: Luke Tinker Press, 1937.

Beck, Mary. *Heroes and Heroines in Tlingit-Haida Legend*. Seattle: Alaska Northwest Books, 1988.

_____. *Shamans and Kushtakas: North Coast Tales of the Supernatural*. Seattle: Alaska Northwest Books, 1991.

Blackman, Margaret. *During My Time: Florence Edenshaw Davidson, A Haida Woman*. Seattle: University of Washington Press, 1982.

Cole, Douglas, and Ira Chaikin. *An Iron Hand Upon the People: The Law Against the Potlatch on the Northwest Coast*. Vancouver, B.C., and Seattle: Douglas and McIntyre and University of Washington Press, 1990.

Corser, H. P. *Totem Lore and Land of the Totem*. Juneau: The Nugget Shop (n.d.).

Dauenhauer, Nora Marks, and Richard Dauenhauer. *Potlatch Oratory*. Seattle: University of Washington Press, 1982.

Emmons, George Thornton. *The Tlingit Indians*. Edited with additions by Frederica de Laguna and a biography by Jean Low. Seattle: University of Washington Press, 1991.

Garfield, Viola, and Linn Forrest. *The Wolf and the Raven: Totem Poles of Southeast Alaska*. Seattle: University of Washington Press, 1956.

Hawthorn, Audrey. *People of the Potlatch*. Vancouver: University of British Columbia Press, 1956.

Hope, Andrew, III. *Raven's Bones*. Sitka Community Association, 1982.

Jonaitis, Aldona. *Chiefly Feasts*. Seattle: University of Washington Press, 1991.

Kamenski, Fr. Anatolii. *Tlingit Indians of Alaska.* Trans. Sergei Kan (1906). Anchorage: University of Alaska Press, 1985.

Kan, Sergei. *Symbolic Immortality, Nineteenth Century Tlingit Potlatch.* Washington, D.C.: The Smithsonian Institution, 1989.

Keithahn, Edward. *Monuments in Cedar.* Seattle: Superior Publishing Company, 1973.

Krause, Aurel. *The Tlingit Indians.* Trans. Erna Gunther. Seattle: University of Washington Press, 1956.

Laguna, Frederica de. *Under Mount St. Elias: The History and Culture of the Yakutat Indians.* Washington, D.C.: The Smithsonian Institution, 1927.

Niblack, Albert P. *The Coast Indians of Southern Alaska and Northern British Columbia.* Washington, D.C.: U.S. National Museum, 1888.

Oberg, Kalvero. *The Social Economy of the Tlingit Indians.* Seattle: University of Washington Press, 1973.

Olson, Ronald L. *Social Structure and Social Life of the Tlingit in Alaska.* Anthropological Records, vol. 26. Berkeley: University of California Press, 1967.

Samuel, Cheryl. *The Chilkat Dancing Blanket.* Seattle: Pacific Search Press, 1982.

_____. *The Raven's Tail.* Vancouver, B.C.: University of British Columbia Press, 1987.

Swanton, John R. *Social Conditions, Beliefs, and Linguistic Relationships of the Tlingit Indians.* Washington, D.C.: Johnson Reprint Corporation, 1970.

_____. *Tlingit Myths and Texts,* Washington, D.C.: Johnson Reprint Corporation, 1970.

ABOUT THE AUTHOR

Mary Giraudo Beck has lived in Ketchikan, Alaska, since 1951, when she married a third-generation Alaskan. Besides rearing a family, she taught literature and writing courses for thirty years at Ketchikan Community College, a branch of the University of Alaska. Mary has an abiding interest in the Native culture of Southeast Alaska and a commitment to recording its oral literature. Previous works include two books, *Heroes and Heroines in Tlingit-Haida Legend* and *Shamans and Kushtakas: North Coast Tales of the Supernatural*, essays on Native mythology, and articles on travel by small boat to towns and Native communities in Southeast Alaska.

ABOUT THE ILLUSTRATOR

Marvin Oliver is an internationally acclaimed contemporary Native American artist who works in metal, glass, wood, and on paper. He teaches Pacific Northwest Coast Indian art at the University of Washington and at the University of Alaska Ketchikan. He is a Seattle resident.